LITERARY HYMNS

LITERARY HYMNS

AN ANTHOLOGY

✛ ✛ ✛

compiled by
MARK BRYANT

Hodder & Stoughton
LONDON · SYDNEY · AUCKLAND

Introduction, collection and biographical notes
copyright © 1999 by Mark Bryant

First published in Great Britain 1999

The right of Mark Bryant to be identified as the Editor of the Work has
been asserted by him in accordance with the Copyright, Designs
and Patents Act 1988

10 9 8 7 6 5 4 3 2 1

British Library Cataloguing in Publication Data
A record for this book is available from
the British Library

ISBN 0 340 72214 2

Printed and bound in Great Britain

Hodder and Stoughton Ltd
A Division of Hodder Headline PLC
338 Euston Road
London NW1 3BH

In Memoriam
Robert John Stanley Bryant (1922–95)

CONTENTS

PREFACE

Alfred, Lord Tennyson once said that 'A good hymn is the most difficult thing in the world to write – you have to be both commonplace and poetical.' The result also has to be, in St Ambrose's definition, a 'song of praise'. However, as many church congregations and school assemblies have borne witness over the ages, combining these elements has sometimes proved a nigh impossible task. The reason has been that, traditionally, many collections of hymns and carols were penned by worthy ecclesiastical figures whose religious credentials greatly outweighed their lyrical skills.

Yet literary hymns do exist and are regularly sung. In fact, a detailed study of hymnbooks compiled over the last two centuries reveals that, though often uncredited, a remarkably large number of poets, writers and scholars have made contributions to this field. For example, it is widely known that William Blake wrote 'Jerusalem' but less so that Christina Rossetti was the author of the popular carol 'In the bleak midwinter' or that it was a fifteen-year-old Milton who composed 'Let us with a gladsome mind'. And students of literature who open their anonymous and dog-eared hymnbooks on Sundays might be surprised to learn that some of the verses before them were written by the likes of Anne and Emily Brontë, Burns, Carlyle, Emerson, Hardy, Ben Jonson, Scott, Walt Whitman, Wordsworth and other such distinguished figures.

Many of these poems were written to be sung as hymns but some have been adapted by others. For instance, the American poet John Greenleaf Whittier once declared 'I know nothing of music and do not claim to have written *one* hymn', yet at least fifty of his verses appear in hymnbooks worldwide, including the celebrated 'Dear Lord and Father of mankind'. And some writers have naturally been more prolific than others: British Prime Minister William Ewart Gladstone (who had once considered the Church as a career before entering politics), wrote only one hymn while Charles Wesley composed some 6,500 in all.

This book, then, is a collection of more than 250 of the best hymns in English written by eminent figures in the worlds of literature and scholarship. By its nature it is very much a personal selection and as a result many favourites may have been omitted through lack of space or copyright availability. However, all the verses published in this anthology have been sung in the form presented here and can be found (often unattributed) in standard hymnbooks, old and new. On occasion the final printed version has varied slightly from the poetic original and where differences occur these have been pointed out in the accompanying notes.

Some of the hymns are translations from Latin, Greek, German etc., but most were originally written in English. They date from the fourth century to the twentieth century and are by male and female authors ranging from royalty, saints, popes, monks and priests to politicians, poets, novelists, scientists and philosophers. Every shade of Christian religious opinion has been represented – whether Catholic or Quaker, Greek Orthodox or Methodist – and the verses have been drawn from a wide variety of nations, from the UK and USA to Italy, Greece, France and Germany.

Finally, I am indebted to the many individuals and institutions who have helped me in my research for this book, not least the staff at the British Library and the Senate House Library, University of London. Particular thanks must also go to my editor, Judith Longman, for her constant encouragement in this project, as well as Julie Ambrose, the designers Penny and Tony Mills, and all the staff at Hodder & Stoughton who have worked so hard to turn it into such an attractive volume.

Mark Bryant
London, 1999

PETER ABELARD

(1079–1142) French theologian

An influential theologian who was declared a heretic by the Council of Sens, Peter Abelard's tragic love-affair with Héloïse was the subject of the poem 'Eloisa to Abelard' by Pope (q. v.). Taken from a hymnbook Abelard wrote for Héloïse's convent, *The Paraclete at Nogent*, this translation is by the celebrated Victorian hymnwriter John Mason Neale.

I

O quanta qualia sunt illa sabbata

O what their joy and their glory must be,
Those endless sabbaths the blessed ones see;
Crown for the valiant, to weary ones rest;
God shall be all and in all ever blest.

What are the monarch, His court and His throne?
What are the peace and the joy that they own?
Tell it, ye blessed, that in it have share,
If what ye feel ye can fully declare.

Truly Jerusalem name we that shore,
Vision of peace, that brings joy evermore;
Wish and fulfilment can severed be ne'er,
Nor the thing prayed for come short of the prayer.

We, whom no trouble distraction can bring,
Safely the anthems of Sion shall sing;
While for Thy grace, Lord, their voices of praise
Thy blessed people shall evermore raise.

There dawns no sabbath; no sabbath is o'er;
Those sabbath-keepers have one and no more;
One and unending is that triumph-song
Which to the angels and us shall belong.

Now, in the meanwhile, with hearts raised on high
We for that country must yearn and must sigh;
Seeking Jerusalem, dear native land,
Through our long exile on Babylon's strand.

Low before Him with our praises we fall,
Of whom and in whom and through whom are all:
Of whom, the Father; and in whom the Son;
Through whom, the Spirit, with these ever one.

✛ ✛ ✛

SARAH FLOWER ADAMS

(1805–48) English poet and hymnwriter

The daughter of radical newspaper editor Benjamin Flower,
Sarah Flower Adams was a friend of Robert Browning (q. v.)
– his love for her sister Eliza allegedly inspired the poem
'Pauline' – and was admired by Leigh Hunt ('a rare mistress of
thought and tears'). This, her most famous hymn, was
reputedly played by the band of the *Titanic* as the ship sank on
14 April 1912.

2

Nearer, my God, to Thee,
    Nearer to Thee!
E'en though it be a cross
    That raiseth me,
Still all my song would be,
'Nearer, my God, to Thee,
    Nearer to Thee!'

Though, like the wanderer,
    The sun gone down,
Darkness be over me,
    My rest a stone,
Yet in my dreams I'd be
Nearer, my God, to Thee,
    Nearer to Thee!

There let the way appear
  Steps unto heaven,
All that Thou send'st to me
  In mercy given,
Angels to beckon me
Nearer, my God, to Thee,
  Nearer to Thee!

Then, with my waking thoughts
  Bright with Thy praise,
Out of my stony griefs
  Bethel I'll raise,
So by my woes to be
Nearer, my God, to Thee,
  Nearer to Thee!

Or if on joyful wing
  Cleaving the sky,
Sun, moon, and stars forgot,
  Upwards I fly,
Still all my song shall be,
  'Nearer, my God, to Thee,
  Nearer to Thee!'

In W. H. Fox, *Hymns and Anthems* (1841)

JOSEPH ADDISON

(1672–1719) English essayist and politician

Son of the Dean of Lichfield, Addison was a Whig MP and
later Chief Secretary to Lord Wharton, Lord Lieutenant of
Ireland. He was married to the Countess of Warwick. Best
known for his essays in the *Spectator* from which these hymns
are taken, Gladstone's Lord Chancellor, Lord Selborne,
thought 'The spacious firmament on high' one of the finest
hymns in the English language.

3

The spacious firmament on high,
With all the blue, ethereal sky,
And spangled heav'ns, a shining frame,
Their great Original proclaim.
Th'unwearied sun, from day to day,
Does his Creator's power display,
And publishes to every land
The work of an Almighty Hand.

Soon as the evening shades prevail,
The moon takes up the wondrous tale,
And nightly to the listening earth
Repeats the story of her birth;
Whilst all the stars that round her burn,
And all the planets in their turn,
Confirm the tidings as they roll,
And spread the truth from pole to pole.

What though, in solemn silence, all
Move round the dark terrestrial ball?
What though nor real voice nor sound
Amid their radiant orbs be found?
In reason's ear they all rejoice,
And utter forth a glorious voice,
For ever singing, as they shine,
'The Hand that made us is Divine'.

From 'Faith and Devotion', *Spectator*, 23 August 1712

4

How are thy servants blest, O Lord!
    How sure is their defence!
Eternal wisdom is their guide,
    Their help omnipotence.

In foreign realms and lands remote,
    Supported by thy care,
Through burning climes they pass unhurt,
    And breathe in tainted air.

From all their griefs and dangers, Lord,
    Thy mercy sets them free,
While in the confidence of prayer
    Their souls take hold on thee.

In midst of dangers, fears, and death,
    Thy goodness we'll adore;
And praise thee for thy mercies past,
    And humbly hope for more.

Our life, while thou preserv'st that life,
    Thy sacrifice shall be;
And death, when death shall be our lot,
    Shall join our souls to thee.

From 'The Wonders of the Deep', *Spectator*, 26 September 1712

5

When all thy mercies, O my God,
    My rising soul surveys,
Transported with the view, I'm lost
    In wonder, love, and praise.

Unnumbered comforts to my soul
    Thy tender care bestowed,
Before my infant heart conceived
    From whence those comforts flowed.

When in the slippery paths of youth
    With heedless steps I ran,
Thine arm, unseen, conveyed me safe,
    And led me up to man.

Through every period of my life
    Thy goodness I'll pursue;
And after death, in distant worlds,
    The glorious theme renew.

When nature fails, and day and night
    Divide thy works no more,
My ever grateful heart, O Lord,
    Thy mercy shall adore.

Through all eternity to thee
    A joyful song I'll raise;
For O! eternity's too short
    To utter all thy praise.

From 'Gratitude', *Spectator*, 9 August 1712

6

The Lord my pasture shall prepare,
And feed me with a shepherd's care;
His presence shall my wants supply,
And guard me with a watchful eye;
My noonday walks he shall attend,
And all my midnight hours defend.

When in the sultry glebe I faint,
Or on the thirsty mountain pant,
To fertile vales and dewy meads
My weary wandering steps he leads,
Where peaceful rivers, soft and slow,
Amid the verdant landscape flow.

Though in a bare and rugged way
Through devious lonely wilds I stray,
Thy bounty shall my pains beguile;
The barren wilderness shall smile
With sudden greens and herbage crowned,
And streams shall murmur all around.

Though in the paths of death I tread,
With gloomy horrors overspread,
My steadfast heart shall fear no ill,
For thou, O Lord, art with me still:
Thy friendly crook shall give me aid,
And guide me through the dreadful shade.

Based on Psalm 23, from 'Divine Providence', *Spectator*, 26 July 1712

ST AMBROSE

(*c.* 340–97) French clergyman

The son of the Prefect of Gaul, Ambrose of Milan was the
greatest bishop of his day and baptised St Augustine. Known
as 'the Father of church song' he introduced Ambrosian chant
and was traditionally believed to have written the 'Te Deum'.

7

Nunc Sancte nobis Spiritus

Come, Holy Ghost, who ever one
Art with the Father and the Son,
Come, Holy Ghost, our souls possess
With thy full flood of holiness.

In will and deed, in heart and tongue,
With all thy powers, thy praise be sung;
And love light up our mortal frame
Till others catch the living flame.

Almighty Father, hear our cry
Through Jesus Christ our Lord most high,
Who with the Holy Ghost and thee
Doth live, and reign eternally.

Translated by Cardinal Newman (q. v.) in his *Verses* (1868)

8

O Lux beata Trinitas

O Trinity, O blessèd Light,
    O Unity, most principal,
The fiery sun now leaves our sight:
    Cause in our hearts thy beams to fall.

Let us with songs of praise divine
    At morn and evening thee implore;
And let our glory, bowed to thine,
    Thee glorify for evermore.

To God the Father, glory great,
    And glory to his only Son,
And to the Holy Paraclete,
    Both now and still while ages run.

Translated by the Royalist poet and friend of Ben Jonson (q. v.),
William Drummond of Hawthornden (1585–1649).

9

Aeterna Christi munera

The eternal gifts of Christ the King,
Apostles' glorious deeds, we sing;
And while due hymns of praise we pay,
Our thankful hearts cast grief away.

The Church in these her princes boasts,
These victor chiefs of warrior hosts;
The soldiers of the heavenly hall,
The lights that rose on earth for all.

'Twas thus the yearning faith of Saints,
The unconquered hope that never faints,
The love of Christ that knows not shame,
The prince of this world overcame.

In them the Father's glory shone,
In them the Spirit's will was done,
The Son himself exults in them;
Joy fills the new Jerusalem.

Redeemer, hear us of thy love,
That, with this glorious band above,
Hereafter, of thine endless grace,
Thy servants also may have place.

Translated by John Mason Neale in *Hymnal Noted* (1852)

10

Aeterne rerum conditor

Framer of the earth and sky,
    Ruler of the day and night,
With a glad variety
    Tempering all, and making light;

Gleams upon our dark path flinging,
    Cutting short each night begun.
Hark! for chanticleer is singing,
    Hark! he chides the lingering sun.

And the morning star replies
    And lets loose the imprisoned day;
And the godless bandit flies
    From his haunt and from his prey.

Shrill it sounds; the storm relenting
    Soothes the weary seaman's ears;
Once it wrought a great repenting
    In that flood of Peter's tears.

Rouse we; let the blithesome cry
    Of that bird our hearts awaken,
Chide the slumberers as they lie,
    And arrest the sin o'ertaken.

Hope and health are in his strain
    To the fearful and the ailing;
Murder sheathes his blade profane;
    Faith revives when faith was failing.

Jesu, Master! when we sin
    Turn on us Thy healing face;
It will melt the offence within
    Into penitential grace.

Beam on our bewildered mind
    Till its dreamy shadows flee:
Stones cry out where Thou hast shined,
    Jesu! musical with Thee.

To the Father and the Son
 And the Spirit, who in heaven
Ever witness, Three in One,
 Praise on earth be ever given.

Translated by Cardinal Newman (q. v.) in his *Verses* (1853)

ST THOMAS AQUINAS
(1227–74) Italian theologian

Best known for his book on scholastic philosophy, *Summa
Theologica*, the celebrated Dominican friar Aquinas was the son
of a Count of Aquino in Italy. His work greatly influenced
Dante's *Divine Comedy*. (For another hymn by Aquinas see under
Gerard Manley Hopkins.)

II

Adore te devote

Thee we adore, O hidden Saviour, thee,
Who in thy Supper with us deign'st to be;
Both flesh and spirit in thy presence fail,
Yet here thy presence we devoutly hail.

O blest memorial of our dying Lord,
Who living bread to men doth here afford!
O may our souls for ever feed on thee,
And thou, O Christ, for ever precious be.

Fountain of goodness, Jesus, Lord and God,
Cleanse us, unclean, in thy most cleansing flood;
Increase our faith and love, that we may know
The hope and peace which from thy presence flow.

O Christ, whom now beneath a veil we see,
May what we thirst for soon our portion be,
To gaze on thee unveiled, and see thy face,
The vision of thy glory and thy grace.

Translated by James Russell Woodford, Bishop of Ely and joint editor
of *The Parish Hymn Book* (1863). From Woodford's *Hymns* (1852).

12

Pange, lingua, gloriosi corporis mysterium

Of the glorious body telling,
   O my tongue, its mysteries sing;
And the blood, all price excelling,
   Which, for this world's ransoming,
In a generous womb once dwelling
   He shed forth, the Gentiles' King.

Given for us, for us descending
   Of a virgin to proceed,
Man with man in converse blending
   Scattered He the gospel seed,
Till His sojourn drew to ending,
   Which He closed in wondrous deed.

At the last great supper seated
   Circled by His brethren's band,
All the law required, completed
   In the feast its statutes planned,
To the twelve Himself He meted
   For their food with His own hand.

Word-made-flesh by word He maketh
   Very bread His flesh to be;
Man in wine Christ's blood partaketh;
   And, if senses fail to see,
Faith alone the true heart waketh
   To behold the mystery.

Therefore we, before it bending,
   This great sacrament adore;
Types and shadows have their ending
   In the new rite evermore:
Faith, our outward sense amending,
   Maketh good defects before.

Honour, laud, and praise addressing
   To the Father and the Son,
Might ascribe we, virtue, blessing,
   And eternal benison:
Holy Ghost, from both progressing,
   Equal laud to Thee be done!

Translated by John Mason Neale in his *Medieval Hymns* (1851)

MATTHEW ARNOLD

(1822–88) English educationalist and poet

The son of the celebrated headmaster of Rugby school, Dr
Thomas Arnold, Matthew Arnold was Private Secretary to the
Marquis of Lansdowne and worked for many years as an
Inspector of Schools. (See also under St Francis of Assisi.)

13

Servants of God, or sons
Shall I not call you, because
Not as servants ye knew
Your father's innermost mind,
His who unwillingly sees
One of his little ones lost.

Yours is the praise if mankind
Hath not as yet in its march
Fainted, and fallen, and died:
A feeble wavering line –
Factions divide them, their host
Threatens to break, to dissolve;

Then, in such hour of need,
Ye, like angels, appear,
Radiant with ardour divine:
Languor is not in your heart,
Weakness is not in your word,
Weariness not on your brow.

Ye alight in our van; at your voice,
Panic, despair, flee away;
Ye move through the ranks, recall
The stragglers, refresh the outworn,
Praise, re-inspire the brave:
Order, courage, return.

Eyes rekindling and prayers
Follow your steps as ye go.
Ye fill up the gaps in our line,
Stablish, continue our march,
On, to the bound of the waste,
On, to the City of God.

Vaughan Williams wrote music specially for this hymn. From Arnold's
'Rugby Chapel' in *New Poems* (1867).

14

Thou, who dost dwell alone –
Thou, who dost know thine own –
Thou, to whom all are known
From the cradle to the grave –
　　Save, oh! save.
From the world's temptations,
　　From tribulations,
From that fierce anguish
Wherein we languish,
From that torpor deep
Wherein we lie asleep,
Heavy as death, cold as the grave,
　　Save, oh! save.

When the soul, growing clearer,
　　Sees God no nearer;
When the soul, mounting higher,
　　To God comes no nigher,
But the arch-fiend Pride
Mounts at her side,
Foiling her high emprise,
Sealing her eagle eyes,
And, when she fain would soar,
Makes idols to adore,
Changing the pure emotion
Of her high devotion,
To a skin-deep sense
Of her own eloquence;
Strong to deceive, strong to enslave –
　　Save, oh! save.

From the ingrained fashion
Of this earthly nature
That mars thy creature;
From grief that is but passion,
From mirth that is but feigning,
From tears that bring no healing,
From wild and weak complaining,
　　Thine old strength revealing,
　　Save, oh! save.

From doubt, where all is double;
Where wise men are not strong,
Where comfort turns to trouble,
Where just men suffer wrong;
Where sorrow treads on joy,
Where sweet things soonest cloy,
Where faiths are built on dust,
Where love is half mistrust,
Hungry, and barren, and sharp as the sea –
        Oh! set us free.

O let the false dream fly,
Where our sick souls do lie
        Tossing continually!
            O where thy voice doth come
            Let all doubts be dumb,
            Let all worlds be mild,
        All strifes be reconciled,
        All pains beguiled!
        Light bring no blindness,
        Love no unkindness,
        Knowledge no ruin,
        Fear no undoing!
            From the cradle to the grave,
            Save, oh! save.

Originally entitled 'Stagirius', this poem was first published in
1849. (Stagirius was a young monk to whom St Chrysostom
            addressed three books.)

ST AUGUSTINE

(354–40) Roman clergyman and theologian

Born in Roman North Africa, St Augustine (not to be confused with St Augustine of Canterbury) became Bishop of Hippo (now Bône, Algeria) and founded the Augustinian sect. Best known as a writer for his *Confessions* and *The City of God*, this hymn is based on a passage in the *Meditations* and is by an anonymous writer 'F.B.P.' (*c.* 1580).

15

Jerusalem, my happy home,
    When shall I come to thee?
When shall my sorrows have an end?
    Thy joys when shall I see?

O happy harbour of the Saints!
    O sweet and pleasant soil!
In thee no sorrow may be found,
    No grief, no care, no toil.

In thee no sickness may be seen,
    No hurt, no ache, no sore;
In thee there is no dread of death,
    But life for evermore.

No dampish mist is seen in thee,
    No cold nor darksome night;
There every soul shines as the sun;
    There God himself gives light.

There lust and lucre cannot dwell;
    There envy bears no sway;
There is no hunger, heat, nor cold,
    But pleasure every way.

Jerusalem, Jerusalem,
    God grant I once may see
Thy endless joys; and of the same
    Partaker aye may be!

Thy walls are made of precious stones,
　　Thy bulwarks diamonds square;
Thy gates are of right orient pearl,
　　Exceeding rich and rare;

Thy turrets and thy pinnacles
　　With carbuncles do shine;
Thy very streets are paved with gold,
　　Surpassing clear and fine;

Thy houses are of ivory,
　　Thy windows crystal clear;
Thy tiles are made of beaten gold—
　　O God that I were there!

Within thy gates no thing doth come
　　That is not passing clean,
No spider's web, no dirt, no dust,
　　No filth may there be seen.

Ah, my sweet home, Jerusalem,
　　Would God I were in thee!
Would God my woes were at an end,
　　Thy joys that I might see!

Thy Saints are crowned with glory great;
　　They see God face to face;
They triumph still, they still rejoice:
　　Most happy is their case.

We that are here in banishment
　　Continually do mourn;
We sigh and sob, we weep and wail,
　　Perpetually we groan.

Our sweet is mixed with bitter gall,
　　Our pleasure is but pain,
Our joys scarce last the looking on,
　　Our sorrows still remain.

But there they live in such delight,
  Such pleasure and such play,
As that to them a thousand years
  Doth seem as yesterday.

Thy vineyards and thy orchards are
  Most beautiful and fair,
Full furnishèd with trees and fruits,
  Most wonderful and rare;

Thy gardens and thy gallant walks
  Continually are green;
There grow such sweet and pleasant flowers
  As nowhere else are seen.

There's nectar and ambrosia made,
  There's musk and civet sweet;
There many a fair and dainty drug
  Is trodden under feet;

There cinnamon, there sugar grows,
  There nard and balm abound—
What tongue can tell, or heart conceive
  The joys that there are found!

Quite through the streets with silver sound
  The flood of life doth flow,
Upon whose banks on every side
  The wood of life doth grow.

There trees for evermore bear fruit,
  And evermore do spring;
There evermore the Angels sit,
  And evermore do sing;

There David stands with harp in hand
  As master of the choir:
Ten thousand times that man were blest
  That might this music hear.

Our Lady sings Magnificat
　　With tune surpassing sweet;
And all the Virgins bear their parts,
　　Sitting about her feet.

Te Deum doth Saint Ambrose sing,
　　Saint Austin doth the like;
Old Simeon and Zachary
　　Have not their songs to seek.

There Magdalene hath left her moan,
　　And cheerfully doth sing
With blessèd Saints, whose harmony
　　In every street doth ring.

Jerusalem, my happy home,
　　Would God I were in thee!
Would God my woes were at an end,
　　Thy joys that I might see!

ANNA LAETITIA BARBAULD

(1743–1825) English writer and journalist

Mrs Barbauld was a poet, editor and (with her brother John
Aikin, Literary Editor of the *Monthly Magazine*) author of
children's books. She was a friend of Hannah More and other
members of the Blue Stocking Circle.

16

Come, said Jesus' sacred voice,
Come, and make my paths your choice!
I will guide you to your home:
Weary pilgrim, hither come!

Thou who, houseless, sole, forlorn,
Long hast borne the proud world's scorn,
Long hast roamed the barren waste,
Weary pilgrim, hither haste!

Ye who, tossed on beds of pain,
Seek for ease but seek in vain,
Ye whose swoln and sleepless eyes
Watch to see the morning rise,

Sinner, come! for here is found
Balm that flows for every wound,
Peace that ever shall endure,
Rest eternal, sacred, sure.

From *Poems* (1792)

17

Praise to God, immortal praise,
For the love that crowns our days!
Bounteous source of every joy,
Let thy praise our tongues employ!

All that Spring with bounteous hand
Scatters o'er the smiling land;
All that liberal Autumn pours
From her rich o'erflowing stores,—

These to thee, my God, we owe,
Source whence all our blessings flow;
And for these my soul shall raise
Grateful vows and solemn praise.

Should thine altered hand restrain
The early and the latter rain,
Blast each opening bud of joy
And the rising year destroy,—

Yet to thee my soul should raise
Grateful vows and solemn praise,
And, when every blessing's flown,
Love thee for thyself alone.

From *Poems* (1773)

SABINE BARING-GOULD

(1834–1924) English clergyman and writer

Once said to have more works listed under his name in the British Library Catalogue than anyone else, the highly prolific Rector of Lew Trenchard, Devon, wrote thirty novels and many books on travel, religion and folklore. His most famous hymn 'Onward Christian soldiers' has been set to music by Haydn and Gustav Holst but the tune specially composed by Sir Arthur Sullivan before he teamed up with W. S. Gilbert remains the most popular.

18

Onward, Christian soldiers!
   Marching as to war,
With the Cross of Jesus
   Going on before.
Christ the royal Master
   Leads against the foe;
Forward into battle,
   See, his banners go!
      Onward, Christian soldiers!
      Marching as to war,
      With the Cross of Jesus
      Going on before.

At the sign of triumph
   Satan's host doth flee;
On then, Christian soldiers,
   On to victory!
Hell's foundations quiver
   At the shout of praise;
Brothers, lift your voices,
Loud your anthems raise.
      Onward, etc.

Like a mighty army
    Moves the Church of God;
Brothers, we are treading
    Where the saints have trod:
We are not divided,
    All one body we,
One in hope and doctrine,
    One in charity.
        Onward, etc.

Crowns and thrones may perish,
    Kingdoms rise and wane,
But the Church of Jesus
    Constant will remain:
Gates of hell can never
    'Gainst that Church prevail;
We have Christ's own promise,
    And that cannot fail.
        Onward, etc.

Onward, then, ye people,
    Join our happy throng,
Blend with ours your voices
    In the triumph song:
Glory, laud, and honour
    Unto Christ the King,
This through countless ages
    Men and angels sing.
        Onward, etc.

First published in *Church Times* (1865)

19

Now the day is over,
    Night is drawing nigh,
Shadows of the evening
    Steal across the sky.

Now the darkness gathers,
    Stars begin to peep,
Birds and beasts and flowers
    Soon will be asleep.

Jesu, give the weary
    Calm and sweet repose;
With thy tenderest blessing
    May mine eyelids close.

Grant to little children
    Visions bright of thee;
Guard the sailors tossing
    On the deep blue sea.

Comfort every sufferer
    Watching late in pain;
Those who plan some evil
    From their sin restrain.

Through the long night watches
    May thine angels spread
Their white wings above me,
    Watching round my bed.

When the morning wakens,
  Then may I arise
Pure and fresh and sinless
  In thy holy eyes.

Glory to the Father,
  Glory to the Son,
And to thee, blest Spirit,
  Whilst all ages run.

First published in *Church Times* (1865)

RICHARD BAXTER
(1615–91) English clergyman and poet

Best known for his book *The Saints' Everlasting Rest*, Baxter was a Puritan during the Civil War but attacked Cromwell for assuming supreme power. He later became Chaplain to Charles II.

20

Ye holy angels bright,
  Who wait at God's right hand,
Or through the realms of light
  Fly at your Lord's command,
    Assist our song,
      Or else the theme
      Too high doth seem
  For mortal tongue.

Ye saints, who toil below,
  Adore your heavenly King,
And onward as ye go
  Some joyful anthem sing;
    Take what he gives,
      And praise him still
      Through good and ill,
  Who ever lives.

Ye blessèd souls at rest,
  Who ran this earthly race,
And now, from sin released,
  Behold the Saviour's face,
    His praises sound,
      As in his sight
      With sweet delight
  Ye do abound.

My soul, bear thou thy part,
  Triumph in God above,
And with a well-tuned heart
  Sing thou the songs of love.
    Let all thy days
      Till life shall end,
      Whate'er he send,
  Be filled with praise.

From 'A Psalm of Praise to the Tune of Psalm cxlviii' in *The Poor Man's Family Book* (1672), rewritten by John Hampden Gurney in *Church Psalmody* (1838)

21

He wants not friends that hath thy love,
   And may converse and walk with thee,
And with thy saints here and above,
   With whom for ever I must be.

In the communion of the saints
   Is wisdom, safety and delight;
And when my heart declines and faints,
   It's raised by their heat and light!

As for my friends, they are not lost;
   The several vessels of thy fleet,
Though parted now, by tempests tossed,
   Shall safely in the haven meet.

Still we are centred all in thee,
   Members, though distant, of one Head;
In the same family we be,
   By the same faith and spirit led.

Before thy throne we daily meet
   As joint petitioners to thee;
In spirit we each other greet,
   And shall again each other see.

The heavenly hosts, world without end,
   Shall be my company above;
And thou, my best and surest Friend,
   Who shall divide me from thy love?

From 'The Resolution' in *Poetical Fragments* (1681)

22

Lord, it belongs not to my care
 Whether I die or live;
To love and serve thee is my share,
 And this thy grace must give.

If life be long, I will be glad
 That I may long obey:
If short, yet why should I be sad
 To welcome endless day?

Christ leads me through no darker rooms
 Than he went through before:
He that unto God's Kingdom comes,
 Must enter by this door.

Come, Lord, when grace hath made me meet
 Thy blessèd face to see;
For if thy work on earth be sweet,
 What will thy glory be!

Then I shall end my sad complaints
 And weary sinful days,
And join with the triumphant saints
 To sing Jehovah's praise.

My knowledge of that life is small,
 The eye of faith is dim;
But 'tis enough that Christ knows all,
 And I shall be with him.

This was reputedly the favourite hymn of James Clerk-Maxwell (1831–79) discoverer of the electro-magnetic nature of light. From 'The Covenant and Confidence of Faith' in *Poetical Fragments* (1681).

THE VENERABLE BEDE
(673–735) English clergyman

Born in Durham, Bede became famous as a scholar at Jarrow Abbey. His most well-known book is the *Historia Ecclesiastica Gentis Anglorum*, a Latin history of the English people from the Roman invasion until the eighth century.

23
Hymnum canamus gloriae

Sing we triumphant hymns of praise,
New hymns to heaven exulting raise:
Christ, by a road before untrod,
Ascendeth to the throne of God.

O grant that we may thither tend,
And with unwearied hearts ascend
Toward thy kingdom's throne, where thou,
Our great high priest, art seated now.

Be thou our joy and strong defence,
Who art our future recompense:
So shall the light that springs from thee
Be ours through all eternity.

O risen Christ, ascended Lord,
All praise to thee let earth accord,
Who art, while endless ages run,
With Father and with Spirit One.

Translated by Benjamin Webb (1819–85) in *Hymnal Noted* (1854)

24

The great forerunner of the morn,
The herald of the Word, is born;
And faithful hearts shall never fail
With thanks and praise his light to hail.

With heavenly message Gabriel came
That John should be that herald's name,
And with prophetic utterance told
His actions great and manifold.

John, still unborn, yet gave aright
His witness to the coming Light;
And Christ, the Sun of all the earth,
Fulfilled that witness at his birth.

Of woman-born shall never be
A greater prophet than was he,
Whose mighty deeds exalt his fame
To greater than a prophet's name.

All praise to God the Father be,
All praise, eternal Son, to thee,
Whom with the Spirit we adore
For ever and for evermore.

Translated by John Mason Neale in *Hymnal Noted* (1854).
(Also translated as 'Hail Harbinger of Morn' by C. S. Calverley.)

ARTHUR CHRISTOPHER BENSON
(1862–1925) English writer

A. C. Benson was the oldest surviving son of E. W. Benson, Archbishop of Canterbury (q. v.), and the brother of the novelists E. F. and R. H. Benson. He was also Master of Magdalene College, Cambridge, and wrote many books and volumes of poetry.

25

O Lord of hosts, who didst upraise
   Strong captains to defend the right
In darker years and sterner days,
   And armedst Israel for the fight:
Thou madest Joshua true and strong,
And David framed the battle-song,

And must we battle yet? Must we,
   Who bear the tender name divine,
Still barter life for victory.
   Still glory in the crimson sign?
The Crucified between us stands,
And lifts on high his wounded hands.

Lord, we are weak and wilful yet,
   The fault is in our clouded eyes;
But thou, through anguish and regret,
   Dost make thy faithless children wise;
Through wrong, through hate, thou dost approve
The far-off victories of love.

And so from out the heart of strife
   Diviner echoes peal and thrill;
The scorned delights, the lavished life,
   The pain that serves a nation's will;
Thy comfort stills the mourner's cries,
And love is crowned by sacrifice.

As rains that weep the clouds away,
　As winds that leave a calm in heaven,
So let the slayer cease to slay,
　Passion be healed, and wrath forgiven;
Draw nearer, bid the tumult cease,
Redeemer, Saviour, Prince of peace!

26

　Lord of grace and holiness,
　Who alone canst guide and bless,
　God of love and tenderness,
　　　Guard these sons of thine.

Jesu, thou wast man indeed,
　Thou dost for our weakness plead,
　Thou dost know our deepest need,
　　　Jesu, keep them thine.

Keep them generous, brave, and true,
Still their loving trust renew,
Make them faithful through and through,
　　　Saviour, keep them thine.

By the words of parting said,
By the tears of sorrow shed
O'er the best belovèd dead,
　　　Father, keep them thine.

By the grace of gentle years,
By all tender hopes and fears,
By the power of loving tears,
　　　Jesu, keep them thine.

Lord, thy loving heart is wide!
Jesu, hold them at thy side,
Saved, redeemed, and sanctified,
　　　Thine, for ever thine!

27

The spring again is here,
    Life wakes from winter's gloom;
In field and forest far and near
    Sweet opening flowerets bloom.

O mystery strange and sweet,
    That life so dumbly bound
Should rise our thankful gaze to greet
    And break from underground.

The morn is fresh and bright,
    The slow, dark hours depart:
Let days unstained and pure delight
    Bring sunshine to the heart.

Lord, touch our careless eyes;
    New life, new ardour bring,
That we may read thy mysteries,
    The wonders of thy spring.

EDWARD WHITE BENSON

(1829–96) English clergyman and writer

A former Headmaster of Wellington College and Bishop of Truro, E. W. Benson became Archbishop of Canterbury in 1883. He edited the *Rugby School Hymn Book* and the *Wellington College Chapel Hymn Book* among other works and was the father of the writers A. C., E. F. and R. H. Benson. As well as writing hymns himself he translated others, such as this one by the French Latin poet, Charles Coffin, Rector of the University of Paris.

28

O Luce qui mortalibus

The splendours of thy glory, Lord,
    Hath no man seen nor known,
And highest angels veil their eyes
    Before thy shining throne.

So bright a day for us prepared,
    For us thou hast in store,
That this all-glorious sun shall fade
    Its sevenfold light before.

When mortal bonds are rent, my God,
    My soul to thee shall soar,
And see thy face, and praise thee well,
    And love thee evermore.

Grant us, O Lord, thy splendid peace,
    Fair love and saintly might;
And on our dim and fleeting day
    Shed thine immortal light.

From Charles Coffin's *Paris Breviary* (1736)

ST BERNARD OF CLAIRVAUX

(1091–1153) French monk

A promoter of the Second Crusade, St Bernard was elected abbot of the Cistercian foundation of Clairvaux, France, at the age of twenty-four. One of the most important figures in the monastic Reformation in the twelfth century, he was an opponent of Abelard (q. v.) whom he condemned as a heretic. Martin Luther (q. v.) called him 'the best monk that ever lived'.

29
Jesu, dulcis memoria

Jesu, the very thought of thee
    With sweetness fills the breast;
But sweeter far thy face to see,
    And in thy presence rest.

Nor voice can sing, nor heart can frame,
    Nor can the memory find
A sweeter sound than Jesu's name,
    O Saviour of mankind.

O hope of every contrite heart,
    O joy of all the meek
To those who ask how kind thou art,
    How good to those who seek!

But what to those who find? Ah! this
    Nor tongue nor pen can show;
The love of Jesus, what it is
    None but his loved ones know.

Jesu, our only joy be thou,
    As thou our prize wilt be
In thee be all our glory now,
    And through eternity.

Translation by Edward Caswall in *The Masque of Mary and Other Poems* (1858)

ST BERNARD OF CLUNY

(12th century) French monk

Believed to have been born of English parents in Morlaix, Brittany, Bernard is best known for his three-thousand-line satirical poem, *De Contemptu Mundi*, which he wrote during his lifetime as a monk at the celebrated Abbey of Cluny.

30

Hic breve vivitur

Brief life is here our portion,
　Brief sorrow, short-lived care:
The life that knows no ending,
　The tearless life, is there.
O happy retribution:
　Short toil, eternal rest;
For mortals and for sinners
　A mansion with the blest!

And now we fight the battle,
　But then shall wear the crown
Of full and everlasting
　And passionless renown.
And now we watch and struggle,
　And now we live in hope,
And Sion in her anguish
　With Babylon must cope.

But he whom now we trust in
　Shall then be seen and known,
And they that know and see him
　Shall have him for their own.
The morning shall awaken,
　The shadows shall decay,
And each true-hearted servant
　Shall shine as doth the day.

There God, our King and portion,
　In fulness of his grace,
Shall we behold for ever,
　And worship face to face.
Then all the halls of Sion
　For ay shall be complete,
And in the Land of Beauty
　All things of beauty meet.

From *De Contemptu Mundi* (*c.* 1145) translated by John Mason Neale

31
Urbs Syon aurea

Jerusalem the golden,
  With milk and honey blest,
Beneath thy contemplation
  Sink heart and voice oppressed:
I know not, O I know not,
  What joys await us there,
What radiancy of glory,
  What light beyond compare.

They stand, those halls of Sion,
  All jubilant with song,
And bright with many an angel,
  And all the martyr throng:
The Prince is ever in them,
  The daylight is serene,
The pastures of the blessèd
  Are decked in glorious sheen.

There is the throne of David,
  And there, from care released,
The song of them that triumph,
  The shout of them that feast;
And they who, with their Leader,
  Have conquered in the fight,
For ever and for ever
  Are clad in robes of white.

O sweet and blessèd country,
  The home of God's elect;
O sweet and blessèd country,
  That eager hearts expect!
Jesu, in mercy bring us
  To that dear land of rest,
Who art, with God the Father,
  And Spirit, ever blest.

From *De Contemptu Mundi* (*c.* 1145) translated by John Mason Neale

32
O bona patria

For thee, O dear, dear country,
  Mine eyes their vigils keep;
For very love, beholding
  Thy happy name, they weep.
The mention of thy glory
  Is unction to the breast,
And medicine in sickness,
  And love and life and rest.

O one, O only mansion!
  O Paradise of joy!
Where tears are ever banished,
  And smiles have no alloy;
The Lamb is all thy splendour,
  The Crucified thy praise;
His laud and benediction
  Thy ransomed people raise.

With jasper glow thy bulwarks,
    Thy streets with emeralds blaze;
The sardius and the topaz
    Unite in thee their rays;
Thine ageless walls are bonded
    With amethyst unpriced;
The saints build up thy fabric,
    Thy Corner-stone is Christ.

Thou hast no shore, fair ocean!
    Thou hast no time, bright day!
Dear fountain of refreshment
    To pilgrims far away.
Upon the Rock of ages
    They raise thy holy tower;
Thine is the victor's laurel,
    And thine the golden dower.

From *De Contemptu Mundi* (*c.* 1145) translated by John Mason Neale

33
Hora novissima

The world is very evil,
    The times are waxing late;
Be sober and keep vigil,
    The Judge is at the gate:
The Judge who comes in mercy,
    The Judge who comes with
        might,
Who comes to end the evil,
    Who comes to crown the right.

O home of fadeless splendour,
    Of flowers that bear no thorn,
Where they shall dwell as children
    Who here as exiles mourn!
'Midst power that knows no limit,
    Where wisdom has no bound,
The beatific vision
    Shall glad the saints around.

Arise, arise, good Christian,
    Let right to wrong succeed;
Let penitential sorrow
    To heavenly gladness lead,
To light that has no evening,
    That knows no moon nor sun,
The light so new and golden,
    The light that is but one.

O happy, holy portion,
    Refection for the blest,
True vision of true beauty,
    True cure of the distrest!
Strive, man, to win that glory;
    Toil, man, to gain that light;
Send hope before to grasp it,
    Till hope be lost in sight.

From *De Contemptu Mundi* (*c.* 1145) translated by John Mason Neale

WILLIAM BLAKE

(1757–1827) English poet and artist

A distinguished poet and artist, many of Blake's verses have been turned into hymns.

34

And did those feet in ancient time
    Walk upon England's mountains green?
And was the holy Lamb of God
    On England's pleasant pastures seen?

And did the countenance divine
    Shine forth upon our clouded hills?
And was Jerusalem builded here
    Among those dark satanic mills?

Bring me my bow of burning gold!
    Bring me my arrows of desire!
Bring me my spear! O clouds, unfold!
    Bring me my chariot of fire!

I will not cease from mental fight,
    Nor shall my sword sleep in my hand,
Till we have built Jerusalem
    In England's green and pleasant land.

Known as 'Jerusalem', this famous hymn is taken from the Preface to
Blake's *Milton* (1804–8)

35

To Mercy, Pity, Peace, and Love
    All pray in their distress,
And to these virtues of delight
    Return their thankfulness.

For Mercy, Pity, Peace, and Love
    Is God our Father dear;
And Mercy, Pity, Peace, and Love
    Is Man, his child and care.

For Mercy has a human heart,   Then every man, of every clime,
    Pity, a human face,   That prays in his distress,
And Love, the human form divine,   Pray to the human form divine.
    And Peace, the human dress.   Love, Mercy, Pity, Peace.

From 'The Divine Image' in *Songs of Innocence* (1789)

36

Can I see another's woe,   And not sit beside the nest,
And not be in sorrow too?   Pouring pity in their breast;
Can I see another's grief,   And not sit the cradle near,
And not seek for kind relief?   Weeping tear on infant's tear;

Can I see a falling tear,   And not sit both night and day
And not feel my sorrow's share?   Wiping all our tears away?
Can a father see his child   O, no! never can it be!
Weep, nor be with sorrow filled?   Never, never can it be!

Can a mother sit and hear   He doth give his joy to all;
An infant groan an infant fear?   He becomes an infant small,
No, No! never can it be!   He becomes a man of woe;
Never, never can it be!   He doth feel the sorrow too.

And can he who smiles on all   Think not thou canst sigh a sigh,
Hear the wren with sorrows small,   And thy maker is not by;
Hear the small bird's grief and care, Think not thou canst weep a tear,
Hear the woes that infants bear,   And thy maker is not near.

              O! he gives to us his joy
              That our grief he may destroy;
              Till our grief is fled and gone,
              He doth sit by us and moan.

'On Another's Sorrow' in *Songs of Innocence* (1789)

ANNE BRONTË

(1820–49) English novelist and poet

Daughter of the Rev. Patrick Brontë, Vicar of Hawarth, Yorkshire, and sister of the novelists Charlotte and Emily (q. v.), Anne Brontë is best known for her books *Agnes Grey* and *The Tenant of Wildfell Hall.* Her hymns appear as poems in a joint pseudonymous publication by the sisters, *Poems by Currer, Ellis and Acton Bell* (1846).

37

Believe not those who say
The upward path is smooth,
Lest thou shouldst stumble in the way
And faint before the truth.

It is the only road
Unto the realms of joy;
But he who seeks that blest abode
Must all his powers employ.

Arm, arm thee for the fight!
Cast useless loads away;
Watch through the darkest hours of night;
Toil through the hottest day.

To labour and to love,
To pardon and endure,
To lift thy heart to God above
And keep thy conscience pure,—

Be this thy constant aim,
Thy hope, thy chief delight;
What matter who should whisper blame,
Or who should scorn or slight,

If but thy God approve,
    And if, within thy breast,
Thou feel the comfort of his love,
    The earnest of his rest.

From 'The Narrow Way' in *Poems by Currer, Ellis and Acton Bell* (1846).
In the original the last verse begins 'What matter, if thy God approve'.

38

Oppressed with sin and woe,
    A burdened heart I bear,
Opposed by many a mighty foe;
    But I will not despair.

With this polluted heart,
    I dare to come to Thee,
Holy and mighty as Thou art;
    For Thou wilt pardon me.

I feel that I am weak,
    And prone to every sin;
But Thou who giv'st to those who seek,
    Wilt give me strength within.

Far as this earth may be
    From yonder starry skies,
Remoter still am I from Thee;
    Yet Thou wilt not despise.

I need not fear my foes,
    I need not yield to care,
I need not sink beneath my woes;
    For Thou wilt answer prayer.

In my Redeemer's name
    I give myself to thee;
And all unworthy as I am,
    My God will cherish me.

Oh, make me wholly Thine!
   Thy love to me impart,
And let Thy holy Spirit shine
   For ever on my heart!

'Confidence' in *Poems by Currer, Ellis and Acton Bell* (1846)

39

My God, (oh, let me call Thee mine,
   Weak, wretched sinner though I be),
My trembling soul would fain be Thine;
   My feeble faith still clings to Thee.

Not only for the past I grieve,
   The future fills me with dismay;
Unless Thou hasten to relieve,
   Thy suppliant is a castaway.

I cannot say my faith is strong,
   I dare not hope my love is great;
But strength and love to Thee belong:
   Oh, do not leave me desolate!

I know I owe my all to Thee;
   Oh, take the heart I cannot give;
Do Thou my Strength, my Saviour be,
   And make me to Thy glory live!

'A Prayer' in *Poems by Currer, Ellis and Acton Bell* (1846)

40

Spirit of Truth! be thou my guide,
   Oh, clasp my hand in thine,
And let me never quit thy side;
   Thy comforts are divine!

Pride scorns thee for thy lowly mien;
   But who like thee can rise
Above this toilsome, sordid scene,
   Beyond the holy skies?

Weak is thine eye and soft thy voice,
   But wondrous is thy might,
To make the wretched soul rejoice,
   To give the simple light!

And still to all that seek thy way
   This magic power is given;
E'en while their footsteps press the clay,
   Their souls ascend to Heaven.

Adapted from 'The Three Guides' in *Poems by Currer, Ellis and
Acton Bell* (1846) by James Martineau (q. v.) for his *Hymns for the
Christian Church and Home*

✥ ✥ ✥

EMILY BRONTË

(1818–48) English novelist and poet

Daughter of the Rev. Patrick Brontë, Vicar of Hawarth,
Yorkshire, and sister of the novelists Charlotte and Anne (q. v.),
Emily Brontë is best known for her book *Wuthering Heights*.

41

No coward soul is mine,
No trembler in the world's storm-troubled sphere:
   I see heaven's glories shine,
And faith shines equal, arming me from fear.

   O God within my breast,
Almighty, ever-present Deity!
   Life – that in me has rest,
As I, undying Life, have power in thee!

Vain are the thousand creeds
That move men's hearts - unutterably vain,
Worthless as withered weeds,
Or idlest froth amid the boundless main,

To waken doubt in one
Holding so fast by thine infinity;
So surely anchored on
The steadfast rock of immortality.

With wide-embracing love
Thy Spirit animates eternal years,
Pervades and broods above,
Changes, sustains, dissolves, creates, and rears.

Though earth and man were gone,
And suns and universes ceased to be,
And thou were left alone,
Every existence would exist in thee.

There is not room for death,
Nor atom that his might could render void:
Thou - thou art Being and Breath,
And what thou art may never be destroyed.

From *Poems by Currer, Ellis and Acton Bell* (1846)

STOPFORD AUGUSTUS BROOKE

(1832–1916) English clergyman and writer

Chaplain to Queen Victoria, Brooke wrote a number of books and after resigning his Holy Orders in 1880 compiled a collection of hymns, *Christian Hymns*, which included a number from his own pen.

42

Let the whole creation cry,
'Glory to the Lord on high!'
Heaven and earth, awake and sing,
'God is good and therefore King.'
Praise him, all ye hosts above,
Ever bright and fair in love;
Sun and moon, uplift your voice,
Night and stars, in God rejoice!

Warriors fighting for the Lord,
Prophets burning with his word,
Those to whom the arts belong,
Add their voices to the song.
Kings of knowledge and of law,
To the glorious circle draw;
All who work and all who wait,
Sing, 'The Lord is good and great!'

Men and women, young and old,
Raise the anthem manifold,
And let children's happy hearts
In this worship bear their parts;
From the north to southern pole
Let the mighty chorus roll:
Holy, holy, holy One,
Glory be to God alone!

Based on Psalm 148, from *Christian Hymns* (1881)

43

It fell upon a summer day,
    When Jesus walked in Galilee,
The mothers from a village brought
    Their children to his knee.

He took them in his arms, and laid
    His hands on each remembered head;
'Suffer these little ones to come
    To me,' he gently said.

'Forbid them not; unless ye bear
    The childlike heart your hearts within,
Unto my Kingdom ye may come,
    But may not enter in.'

Master, I fain would enter there;
    O let me follow thee, and share
Thy meek and lowly heart, and be
    Freed from all worldly care.

Of innocence, and love, and trust
    Of quiet work, and simple word,
Of joy, and thoughtlessness of self,
    Build up my life, good Lord.

All happy thoughts, and gentle ways,
    And loving-kindness daily given,
And freedom through obedience gained,
    Make in my heart thy heaven.

O happy thus to live and move!
    And sweet this world, where I shall find
God's beauty everywhere, his love,
    His good in all mankind.

Then, Father, grant this childlike heart,
    That I may come to Christ, and feel
His hands on me in blessing laid,
    Love-giving, strong to heal.

From *Christian Hymns* (1881)

SIR THOMAS BROWNE

(1605–82) English physician and writer

Knighted by Charles II, Sir Thomas Browne practised medicine for most of his life but also wrote many scientific and antiquarian works. He is best known for his book *Religio Medici* (1642) from which this hymn is taken. Vaughan Williams composed a tune especially for it.

44

The night is come, like to the day,
Depart not thou, great God, away.
Let not my sins, black as the night,
Eclipse the lustre of thy light.

O thou, whose nature cannot sleep,
Upon my temples sentry keep;
And guard me 'gainst those watchful foes
Whose eyes are open while mine close.

O let no dreams my head infest,
But such as Jacob's temples blest.
While I do rest, my soul advance;
And make my sleep a holy trance.

That so I may, my rest being wrought,
Awake into some holy thought,
And with as active vigour run
My course, as doth the nimble sun.

Sleep is a death: O make me try,
By sleeping, what it is to die!
And then as gently lay my head
Upon my grave, as now my bed.

Howe'er I rest, great God, let me
Awake again at last with thee;
And thus assured, behold I lie
Securely, or to wake or die.

✛ ✛ ✛

ELIZABETH BARRETT BROWNING

(1806–61) English poet

Already established as a major poet before meeting her future husband, Robert Browning (q. v.) – so much so that she was suggested as a possible Poet Laureate on the death of Wordsworth (q. v.) – a number of Elizabeth Barrett Browning's poems have been adapted as hymns.

45

Of all the thoughts of God that are
Borne inward into souls afar,
Along the Psalmist's music deep,
Now tell me if that any is,
For gift or grace, surpassing this:
'He giveth His belovèd – sleep'?

What would we give to our beloved?
The hero's heart to be unmoved,
The poet's star-tuned harp to sweep,
The patriot's voice to teach and rouse,
The monarch's crown to light the brows?
He giveth His belovèd – sleep.

What do we give to our beloved?
A little faith all undisproved,
A little dust to overweep,
And bitter memories to make
The whole earth blasted for our sake:
He giveth His belovèd – sleep.

'Sleep soft, beloved!' we sometimes say,
Who have no tune to charm away
Sad dreams that through the eyelids creep:
But never doleful dream again
Shall break the happy slumber when
He giveth His belovèd – sleep.

O earth, so full of dreary noises !
O men, with wailing in your voices!
O delvèd gold, the wailers heap!
O strife, O curse, that o'er it fall!
God strikes a silence through you all,
And giveth His belovèd – sleep.

His dews drop mutely on the hill,
His cloud above it saileth still,
Though on its slope men sow and reap:
More softly than the dew is shed,
Or cloud is floated overhead,
He giveth His belovèd – sleep.

Ay, men may wonder while they scan
A living, thinking, feeling man
Confirmed in such a rest to keep;
But angels say, and through the word
I think their happy smile is *heard* –
'He giveth His belovèd – sleep.'

For me, my heart that erst did go
Most like a tired child at a show,
That sees through tears the mummers leap,
Would now its wearied vision close,
Would childlike on His love repose
Who giveth His belovèd – sleep.

And friends, dear friends, when it shall be
That this low breath is gone from me,
And round my bier ye come to weep,
Let One, most loving of you all,
Say 'Not a tear must o'er her fall!
He giveth His belovèd sleep.'

'The Sleep' (the line 'He giveth His beloved sleep' comes
from Psalm 127)

46

How high Thou art! our songs can own
　　No music Thou couldst stoop to hear!
But still the Son's expiring groan
　　Is vocal in the Father's ear.

How pure Thou art! our hands are dyed
　　With curses, red with murder's hue–
But He hath stretched His hands to hide
　　The sins that pierced them from Thy view.

How strong Thou art! we tremble lest
　　The thunders of Thine arm be moved–
But He is lying on Thy breast,
　　And Thou must clasp Thy best Beloved!

How kind Thou art! Thou didst not choose
　　To joy in Him for ever so;
But that embrace Thou wilt not loose
　　For vengeance, didst for love forego!

High God, and pure, and strong, and kind!
　　The low, the foul, the feeble, spare!
Thy brightness in His face we find–
　　Behold our darkness only *there*!

'The Mediator'

47

When Jesus' friend had ceased to be,
　　Still Jesus' heart its friendship kept–
'Where have ye laid him?' – 'Come and see!'
　　But ere His eyes could see, they wept.

Lord! not in sepulchres alone,
　　Corruption's worm is rank and free;
The shroud of death our bosoms own–
　　The shades of sorrow! Come and see!

Come, Lord! God's image cannot shine
   Where sin's funereal darkness lowers–
Come! turn those weeping eyes of Thine
   Upon these sinning souls of ours!

And let those eyes, with shepherd care,
   Their moving watch above us keep;
Till love the strength of sorrow wear,
   And as Thou weepedst, *we* may weep!

For surely we may weep to know,
   So dark and deep our spirit's stain;
That had Thy blood refused to flow,
   Thy very tears had flowed in vain.

        'The Weeping Saviour'

48

God, namèd Love, whose fount Thou art,
   Thy crownless Church before Thee stands,
With too much hating in her heart,
   And too much striving in her hands!

O loving Lord ! O slain for love
   Thy blood upon Thy garments came–
Inwrap their folds our brows above,
   Before we tell Thee all our shame!

'Love as I loved you,' was the sound
   That on Thy lips expiring sate!
Sweet words, in bitter strivings drowned!
   We hated as the worldly hate.

The spear that pierced for love Thy side,
   We dared for wrathful use to crave;
And with our cruel noise denied
   Its silence to Thy blood-red grave!

Ah, blood! that speaketh more of love
    Than Abel's–could we speak like Cain,
And grieve and scare that holy Dove,
    The parting love-gift of the Slain?

Yet, Lord, Thy wrongèd love fulfil!
    Thy Church, though fallen, before Thee stands–
Behold, the voice is Jacob's still,
    Albeit the hands are Esau's hands!

Hast Thou no tears, like those besprent
    Upon Thy Zion's ancient part?
No moving looks, like those which sent
    Their softness through a traitor's heart?

No touching tale of anguish dear;
    Whereby like children we may creep,
All trembling, to each other near,
    And view each other's face, and weep?

Oh, move us–Thou hast power to move–
    One in the one Beloved to be!
Teach us the heights and depths of love–
    Give Thine–that we may love like Thee!

'A Supplication for Love'

ROBERT BROWNING

(1812–89) English poet and dramatist

Himself a distinguished poet and playwright, Robert Browning admired the verses of and later married Elizabeth Barrett Browning (q. v.).

49

The year's at the spring,
    And day's at the morn;
Morning's at seven;
    The hill-side's dew-pearled;
The lark's on the wing;
    The snail's on the thorn;
God's in his heaven–
    All's right with the world!

From *Pippa Passes* (1841)

50

There's heaven above, and night by night
    I look right through its gorgeous roof;
No suns and moons though e'er so bright
    Avail to stop me; splendour-proof,
    I keep the brood of stars aloof.

For I intend to get to God,
    For 'tis to God I speed so fast,
For in God's breast, my own abode,
    Those shoals of dazzling glory passed,
    I lay my spirit down at last.

I lie where I have always lain,
    God smiles as he has always smiled;
Ere suns and moons could wax and wane,
    Ere stars were thundergirt, or piled
    The heavens, God thought on me his child.

God, whom I praise: how could I praise,
    If such as I might understand,
Make out and reckon on his ways,
    And bargain for his love, and stand,
    Paying a price, at his right hand!

From *Bells and Pomegranates III* (1842)

51

  Then welcome each rebuff
  That turns earth's smoothness rough,
Each sting that bids nor sit nor stand but go!
    Be our joys three parts pain!
    Strive, and hold cheap the strain;
Learn, nor account the pang; dare, never grudge the throe!

    Yet gifts should prove their use:
    I own the Past profuse
Of power each side, perfection every turn:
    Eyes, ears took in their dole,
    Brain treasured up the whole;
Should not the heart beat once 'How good to live and learn!'

    Not once beat 'Praise be thine!
    I see the whole design,
I who saw power, see now love perfect too:
    Perfect I call thy plan:
    Thanks that I was a man!
Maker, remake, complete; I trust what thou shalt do.'

    So, take and use thy work!
    Amend what flaws may lurk,
What strain o' the stuff, what warpings past the aim!
    My times be in thy hand!
    Perfect the cup as planned!
Let age approve of youth, and death complete the same!

From 'Rabbi Ben Ezra' in *Dramatis Personae* (1864)

✤ ✤ ✤

WILLIAM CULLEN BRYANT
(1794–1878) American poet and journalist

For fifty years editor of the *New York Evening Post*, W. C. Bryant
was the founder of American poetry.

52

O God, whose dread and dazzling brow
    Love never yet forsook,
On those who seek thy presence now,
    In deep compassion look.

For many a frail and erring heart
    Is in thy holy sight,
And feet too willing to depart
    From the plain way of right.

Yet, pleased the humble prayer to hear
    And kind to all that live,
Thou, when thou seest the contrite tear,
    Art ready to forgive.

53

O North, with all thy vales of green,
    O South, with all thy palms,
From peopled towns and fields between
    Uplift the voice of psalms:
Raise, ancient East, the anthem high,
And let the youthful West reply.

Lo! in the clouds of heaven appears
    God's well-belovèd Son;
He brings a train of brighter years,
    His kingdom is begun!
He comes a guilty world to bless
With mercy, truth and righteousness.

O Father, haste the promised hour,
    When at his feet shall lie
All rule, authority, and power
    Beneath the ample sky,
And he shall reign from pole to pole
The Lord of every human soul;

When all shall heed the words he said,
    Amid their daily cares,
And by the loving life he led
    Shall strive to pattern theirs.
And he, who conquered death, shall win
The mightier conquest over sin.

54

O thou, whose own vast temple stands,
    Built over earth and sea!
Accept the walls that human hands
    Have raised to worship thee.

Lord! from thine inmost glory send
    Within these courts to bide,
The peace that dwelleth without end
    Serenely by thy side.

May erring minds that worship here
    Be taught the better way;
And they who mourn, and they who fear,
    Be strengthened as they pray.

May faith grow firm, and love grow warm,
    And pure devotion rise,
While round these hallowed walls the storm
    Of earth-born passion dies.

JOHN BUNYAN

(1628–88) English clergyman and writer

John Bunyan began writing his most famous book, *The Pilgrim's Progress*, in Bedford Prison where he had been sent for preaching without a licence.

55

Who would true valour see,
    Let him come hither;
One here will constant be,
    Come wind, come weather;
There's no discouragement
Shall make him once relent
His first avowed intent
      To be a pilgrim.

Who so beset him round
    With dismal stories
Do but themselves confound;
    His strength the more is.
No lion can him fright;
He'll with a giant fight;
But he will have a right
      To be a pilgrim.

Hobgoblin nor foul fiend
    Can daunt his spirit;
He knows he at the end
    Shall life inherit.
Then fancies fly away,
He'll fear not what men say;
He'll labour night and day
    To be a pilgrim.

From *The Pilgrim's Progress* (1684). The hobgoblins were removed and
the first line changed to 'He who would valiant be' by the editors of
the *English Hymnal* (1904)

56

Blest be the day that I began
    A pilgrim for to be;
And blessèd also be that man
    That thereto movèd me.

'Tis true, 'twas long ere I began
    To seek to live for ever;
But now I run fast as I can;
    'Tis better late than never.

Some of the ditch shy are, yet can
    Lie tumbling in the mire;
Some, though they shun the frying pan,
    Do leap into the fire.

What danger is the pilgrim in,
    How many are his foes!
How many ways there are to sin
    No living mortal knows.

The Lord is only my support
    And he that doth me feed;
How can I then want anything
    Whereof I stand in need?

Our tears to joy, our fears to faith,
    Are turnèd as we see,
That our beginning, as one saith,
    Shows what our end will be.

From *The Pilgrim's Progress* (1684)

57

He that is down needs fear no fall,
    He that is low, no pride;
He that is humble ever shall
    Have God to be his guide.

I am content with what I have,
    Little be it, or much:
And, Lord, contentment still I crave,
    Because thou savest such.

Fullness to such, a burden is,
    That go on pilgrimage:
Here little, and hereafter bliss,
    Is best from age to age.

From *The Pilgrim's Progress* (1684)

✠ ✠ ✠

ROBERT BURNS
(1759–96) Scottish poet

A number of the poems of the 'Heaven-taught ploughman'
from Ayrshire have been turned into hymns, some of them
being included in collections such as *Hymns for the Christian
Church and Home* by James Martineau (q. v.).

58

O Thou, the first, the greatest friend
    Of all the human race!
Whose strong right hand has ever been
    Their stay and dwelling place!

Before the mountains heav'd their heads
    Beneath Thy forming hand,
Before this ponderous globe itself
    Arose at Thy command:

That Power, which rais'd and still upholds
    This universal frame,
From countless, unbeginning time
    Was ever still the same.

Those mighty periods of years,
    Which seem to us so vast,
Appear no more before Thy sight
    Than yesterday that's past.

Thou giv'st the word: Thy creature, man,
    Is to existence brought;
Again Thou say'st: 'Ye sons of men,
    Return ye into nought!'

Thou layest them, with all their cares,
    In everlasting sleep;
As with a flood Thou tak'st them off
    With overwhelming sweep.

They flourish like the morning flower
   In beauty's pride array'd,
But long ere night, cut down, it lies
   All wither'd and decay'd.

'The Ninetieth Psalm Versified'. Martineau changed verse six to read
'Thou lay'st them fast, with all their cares, /In adamantine sleep'.

59

O Thou unknown, Almighty Cause
   Of all my hope and fear!
In whose dread presence, ere an hour,
   Perhaps I must appear!

If I have wander'd in those paths
   Of life I ought to shun–
As something, loudly, in my breast,
   Remonstrates I have done–

Thou know'st that Thou hast formèd me
   With passions wild and strong;
And list'ning to their witching voice
   Has often led me wrong.

Where human weakness has come short,
   Or frailty stept aside,
Do Thou, All-good – for such Thou art –
   In shades of darkness hide.

Where with intention I have err'd,
   No other plea I have,
But, Thou art good; and Goodness still
   Delighteth to forgive.

'A Prayer in the Prospect of Death', from *Poems* (1786)

✠ ✠ ✠

JOHN BYROM
(1692–1763) English poet

Inventor of a popular system of shorthand, Byrom was a Fellow of the Royal Society and a friend of the Wesleys (q. v.), but is perhaps best known for his hymn 'Christians awake! salute the happy morn' which was written for his daughter Dolly as a Christmas present in 1749.

60

Christians, awake! salute the happy morn,
Whereon the Saviour of the world was born;
Rise to adore the mystery of love,
Which hosts of angels chanted from above:
With them the joyful tidings first begun
Of God incarnate and the Virgin's Son.

Then to the watchful shepherds it was told,
Who heard the angelic herald's voice, 'Behold,
I bring good tidings of a Saviour's birth
To you and all the nations upon earth:
This day hath God fulfilled his promised word,
This day is born a Saviour, Christ the Lord.'

He spake; and straightway the celestial choir
In hymns of joy, unknown before, conspire;
The praises of redeeming love they sang,
And heaven's whole orb with Alleluias rang:
God's highest glory was their anthem still,
Peace upon earth, and unto men good will.

To Bethlehem straight the enlightened shepherds ran,
To see the wonder God had wrought for man,
And found, with Joseph and the blessèd Maid,
Her Son, the Saviour, in a manger laid:
Then to their flocks, still praising God, return,
And their glad hearts with holy rapture burn.

O may we keep and ponder in our mind
God's wondrous love in saving lost mankind;
Trace we the Babe, who hath retrieved our loss,
From his poor manger to his bitter Cross;
Tread in his steps, assisted by his grace,
Till man's first heavenly state again takes place.

Then may we hope the angelic hosts among,
To sing, redeemed, a glad triumphal song:
He that was born upon this joyful day
Around us all his glory shall display;
Saved by his love, incessant we shall sing
Erternal praise to heaven's almighty King.

From *Poems* (1773)

61

My spirit longs for thee
   Within my troubled breast,
Though I unworthy be
   Of so divine a guest.

Of so divine a guest
   Unworthy though I be,
Yet has my heart no rest
   Unless it come from thee.

Unless it come from thee,
   In vain I look around;
In all that I can see
   No rest is to be found.

No rest is to be found
   But in thy blessèd love:
O let my wish be crowned,
   And send it from above!

From *Poems* (1773)

THOMAS CAMPBELL

(1777–1844) English poet

A friend of Sir Walter Scott (q. v.) Campbell is best remembered today for his battle poems and ballads.

62

Men of England, who inherit
   Rights that cost your sires their blood!
Men whose undegenerate spirit
   Has been proved on field and flood.

Yet, remember, England gathers
   Hence but fruitless wreaths of fame,
If the freedom of your fathers
   Glow not in your hearts the same.

What are monuments of bravery,
   Where no public virtues bloom?
What avail in lands of slavery
   Trophied temples, arch and tomb?

We're the sons of sires that baffled
   Crowned and mitred tyranny;
They defied the field and scaffold
   For their birthrights–so will we!

From *The New Monthly Magazine* (1822)

THOMAS CAMPION

(1567–1620) English physician, poet and dramatist

A practising doctor, Thomas Campion (or Campian) was also an accomplished musician, poet and playwright, writing in Latin and English, and his masques were performed before James I. He wrote both the words and the music to his hymns.

63

Lift up to heav'n, sad wretch, thy heavy sprite,
    What though thy sins thy due destruction threat?
The Lord exceeds in mercy as in might:
    His ruth is greater, though thy crimes be great.

Repentance needs not fear the heaven's just rod,
    It stays even thunder in the hand of God.
With cheerful voice to him then cry for grace;
    Thy faith and fainting hope with prayer revive.

Remorse for all that truly mourn hath place;
    Not God, but men of him themselves deprive.
Strive then and he will help. Call him, he'll hear:
    The son needs not the Father's fury fear.

64

Sing a song of joy, praise our God with mirth.
His flock who can destroy? Is he not Lord of heaven and earth?

Sing we then secure, tuning well our strings,
With voice as echo pure, let us renown the King of Kings.

First who taught the day from the east to rise?
Whom doth the sun obey when in the seas his glory dies?

He the stars directs that in order stand:
Who heaven and earth protects but he that framed them with his hand?

All that dread his name, and his hests observe,
His arm will shield from shame, their steps from truth shall never
   swerve.

Let us then rejoice, sounding loud his praise,
So will he hear our voice, and bless on earth our peaceful days.

             From *Two Bookes of Ayres* (*c.* 1613)

65

  Never weather-beaten sail more willingly bent to shore,
  Never tired pilgrim's limbs affected slumber more,
  Than my wearied sprite now longs to fly out of my troubled breast.
  O come quickly, sweetest Lord, and take my soul to rest.

  Ever blooming are the joys of heaven's high paradise,
  Cold age deafs not there our ears, nor vapour dims our eyes;
  Glory there the sun outshines, whose beams the blessèd only see;
  O come quickly, glorious Lord, and raise my sprite to thee.

             From *Two Bookes of Ayres* (*c.* 1613)

66

  View me, Lord, a work of thine:
    Shall I then lie drowned in night?
  Might thy grace in me but shine,
    I should seem made all of light.

  Cleanse me, Lord, that I may kneel
    At thine altar, pure and white:
  They that once thy mercies feel
    Gaze no more on earth's delight.

  Worldly joys, like shadows, fade
    When the heavenly light appears;
  But the covenants thou hast made,
    Endless, know nor days nor years.

In thy word, Lord, is my trust;
   To thy mercies fast I fly;
Though I am but clay and dust,
   Yet thy grace can lift me high.

✠ ✠ ✠

THOMAS CARLYLE

(1795–1881) Scottish historian and writer

A Presbyterian by upbringing, Carlyle studied at first for the ministry but later decided on literature as a profession, producing such celebrated works as *History of the French Revolution*, *Frederick the Great* and *Sartor Resartus*. He also wrote the best known translation of the famous hymn 'Ein feste Burg' by Martin Luther (q. v.).

67

So here hath been dawning
   Another blue day.
Think, wilt thou let it
   Slip useless away?

Out of eternity
   This new day is born;
Into eternity,
   At night, will return.

Behold it aforetime
   No eye ever did:
So soon it for ever
   From all eyes is hid.

Here hath been dawning
   Another blue day.
Think, wilt thou let it
   Slip useless away?

From *Miscellaneous Essays*

CHARLEMAGNE

(742–814) King of the Franks and Holy Roman Emperor

Crowned the first Holy Roman Emperor by Pope Leo III, Charlemagne's exploits feature in *The Song of Roland*. The influential English theologian Alcuin was a member of his court. This hymn has been attributed to him (see also the translation by Dryden).

68

Veni, Creator Spiritus

Come, Holy Ghost, our souls inspire
And lighten with celestial fire:
Thou the anointing Spirit art,
Who dost thy sevenfold gifts impart:
Thy blessed unction from above
Is comfort, life, and fire of love.

Enable with perpetual light
The dullness of our blinded sight:
Anoint and cheer our soilèd face
With the abundance of thy grace;
Keep far our foes, give peace at home;
Where thou art guide no ill can come.

Teach us to know the Father, Son,
And thee, of both, to be but One;
That through the ages all along
This may be our endless song;
Praise to thy eternal merit,
Father, Son, and Holy Spirit.

Translated by Bishop John Cosin in his *Collection of Private Devotions* (1627). It also occurs in the *Book of Common Prayer* (1662), in the final revision of which Cosin took part.

THOMAS CHATTERTON
(1752–70) English poet

This young English poet, who committed suicide aged only seventeen, nonetheless produced a considerable amount of verse, the best known being his 'Rowley' poems purporting to be the work of a fifteenth-century Bristol monk.

69

O God, Whose thunder shakes the sky,
   Whose eye this atom globe surveys,
To Thee, my only rock, I fly
   Thy mercy in Thy justice praise.

The mystic mazes of Thy will,
   The shadows of celestial light,
Are past the power of human skill,–
   But what the Eternal does is right.

O teach me in the trying hour,
   When anguish swells the dewy tear,
To still my sorrows, own Thy power,
   Thy goodness love, Thy justice fear.

The gloomy mantle of the night,
   Which on my sinking spirit steals,
Will vanish at the morning light
   Which God, my orient sun reveals.

From 'The Resignation' as printed in Martineau's *Hymns* (q. v.). The original version is longer, has 'acts is right' at the end of the second verse and the last line reads 'Which God, my East, my Sun, reveals'.

JOHN CLARE
(1793–1864) English poet

A rural poet from Northamptonshire, John Clare was admitted to a mental asylum in Epping in 1837, escaped in 1841, and walked home to Northampton where he was later reinterned for the rest of his life.

70

A stranger once did bless the earth
    Who never caused a heart to mourn,
Whose very voice gave sorrow mirth–
    And how did earth his worth return?
It spurned him from its lowliest lot,
The meanest station owned him not.

An outcast thrown in sorrow's way,
    A fugitive that knew no sin,
Yet in lone places forced to stray–
    Men would not take the stranger in.
Yet peace, though much himself he mourned,
Was all to others he returned.

His presence was a peace to all,
    He bade the sorrowful rejoice.
Pain turned to pleasure at his call,
    Health lived and issued from his voice;
He healed the sick, and sent abroad
The dumb rejoicing in the Lord.

The blind met daylight in his eye,
    The joys of everlasting day;
The sick found health in his reply;
    The cripple threw his crutch away.
Yet he with troubles did remain,
And suffered poverty and pain.

It was for sin he suffered all
   To set the world-imprisoned free,
To cheer the weary when they call–
   And who could such a stranger be?
The God, who hears each human cry,
And came, a Saviour, from on high.

✢ ✢ ✢

ARTHUR HUGH CLOUGH

(1819–61) English poet and academic

Successively Fellow of Oriel College, Oxford, and Warden of University Hall, London, Clough later went to America where he became a friend of Emerson (q. v.), returning to England in 1853 as an Examiner in the Education Office.

71

Say not, 'The struggle nought availeth,
   The labour and the wounds are vain,
The enemy faints not, nor faileth,
   And as things have been they remain.'

If hopes were dupes, fears may be liars;
   It may be, in yon smoke concealed,
Your comrades chase e'en now the fliers,
   And, but for you, possess the field.

For while the tired waves, vainly breaking,
   Seem here no painful inch to gain,
Far back, through creeks and inlets making,
   Comes silent, flooding in, the main.

And not by eastern windows only,
   When daylight comes, comes in the light;
In front the sun climbs slow, how slowly,
   But westward, look, the land is bright!

From Poems (1863)

SAMUEL TAYLOR COLERIDGE

(1772–1834) English poet and lay preacher

S. T. Coleridge was the son of the Vicar of Ottery St Mary, Devon, and later himself considered entering the Unitarian ministry, travelling widely thoughout the West Country as a lay preacher.

72

O sweeter than the marriage-feast,
   'Tis sweeter far to me,
To walk together to the kirk
   With a goodly company;

To walk together to the kirk
   And all together pray:
Old men and babes and loving friends
   And youths and maidens gay.

He prayeth well, who loveth well
   Both man and bird and beast;
And he that loveth all God made
   That man he prayeth best.

He prayeth best, who loveth best
   All things both great and small;
For the dear God who loveth us
   He made and loveth all.

From The Ancient Mariner (1798)
73

Ere on my bed my limbs I lay,
God grant me grace my prayers to say:
O God! preserve my mother dear
In strength and health for many a year;
And, O! preserve my father too,
And may I pay him reverence due;
And may I my best thoughts employ
To be my parents' hope and joy;
And O! preserve my brothers both
From evil doings and from sloth,
And may we always love each other
Our friends, our father, and our mother:
And still, O Lord, to me impart
An innocent and grateful heart,
That after my great sleep I may
Awake to thy eternal day!

'A Child's Evening Prayer' (1852)

ST COLUMBA

(521–97) Irish missionary

Born in County Donegal, St Columba is best known as the founder of the monastery on the island of Iona in Scotland.

74

Christus Redemptor gentium

Christ is the world's Redeemer,
   The lover of the pure,
The fount of heav'nly wisdom,
   Our trust and hope secure;
The armour of his soldiers,
   The Lord of earth and sky;
Our health while we are living,
   Our life when we shall die.

Christ hath our host surrounded
   With clouds of martyrs bright,
Who wave their palms in triumph,
   And fire us for the fight.
For Christ the cross ascended
   To save a world undone,
And, suffering for the sinful,
   Our full redemption won.

Down in the realm of darkness
   He lay a captive bound,
But at the hour appointed
   He rose, a Victor crowned;
And now, to heav'n ascended,
   He sits upon the throne,
In glorious dominion,
   His Father's and his own.

Glory to God the Father,
   The unbegotten One;
All honour be to Jesus,
   His sole-begotten Son;
And to the Holy Spirit–
   The perfect Trinity,
Let all the worlds give answer,
   'Amen - so let it be'.

Translated by Duncan MacGregor (1854–1923)

MILES COVERDALE

(1487–1568) English clergyman and translator

A Lutheran priest, and later Bishop of Exeter, Miles Coverdale's fame rests on his translation of the Bible into English from German and Latin.

75

I call on the Lord Jesu Christ,
   I have none other help but thee.
My heart is never set at rest
   Till thy sweet word have comforted me.

A steadfast faith grant me therefore,
   To hold by thy word evermore
Above all thing, never resisting,
   But to increase in faith more and more.

From *Goostly Psalmes and Spritualle Songes* (*c.* 1546)

WILLIAM COWPER

(1731–1800) English poet

Son of the Rector of Great Berkhamsted (a chaplain to George II), and brother of Earl Cowper, Lord Chancellor, Cowper suffered from fits of depression and lived for a time with the Rev. Morley Unwin in Huntingdon before moving to Olney where he became close friends with the local curate, John Newton (q. v.), with whom he wrote the famous *Olney Hymns*.

76

God moves in a mysterious way
　　His wonders to perform;
He plants his footsteps in the sea,
　　And rides upon the storm.

Deep in unfathomable mines
　　Of never-failing skill
He treasures up his bright designs,
　　And works his sovereign will.

Ye fearful saints, fresh courage take;
　　The clouds ye so much dread
Are big with mercy, and will break
　　In blessings on your head.

Judge not the Lord by feeble sense,
　　But trust him for his grace:
Behind a frowning providence
　　He hides a smiling face.

His purposes will ripen fast,
　　Unfolding every hour;
The bud may have a bitter taste,
　　But sweet will be the flower.

Blind unbelief is sure to err,
　　And scan his work in vain;
God is his own interpreter,
　　And he will make it plain.

From *Olney Hymns* (1779)

77

Sometimes a light surprises
　　The Christian while he sings:
It is the Lord who rises
　　With healing in his wings;
When comforts are declining,
　　He grants the soul again
A season of clear shining
　　To cheer it after rain.

In holy contemplation
　　We sweetly then pursue
The theme of God's salvation,
　　And find it ever new:
Set free from present sorrow,
　　We cheerfully can say,
E'en let the unknown morrow
　　Bring with it what it may,

It can bring with it nothing
    But he will bear us through;
Who gives the lilies clothing
    Will clothe his people too:
Beneath the spreading heavens
    No creature but is fed;
And he who feeds the ravens
    Will give his children bread.

Though vine nor fig-tree neither
    Their wonted fruit should bear,
Though all the fields should wither,
    Nor flocks nor herds be there;
Yet, God the same abiding,
    His praise shall tune my voice;
For, while in him confiding,
    I cannot but rejoice.

From 'Joy and Peace in Believing' in *Olney Hymns* (1779), Francis
Palgrave (q.v.) described this hymn as 'This brilliant Lyric'.

78

O for a closer walk with God,
    A calm and heavenly frame,
A light to shine upon the road
    That leads me to the Lamb!

Where is the blessedness I knew
    When first I saw the Lord?
Where is the soul-refreshing view
    Of Jesus and his word?

What peaceful hours I once enjoy'd!
    How sweet their mem'ry still!
But they have left an aching void
    The world can never fill.

Return, O holy Dove, return,
    Sweet messenger of rest;
I hate the sins that made thee mourn
    And drove thee from my breast.

The dearest idol I have known,
    Whate'er that idol be,
Help me to tear it from thy throne,
    And worship only thee.

So shall my walk be close with God
　　Calm and serene my frame;
So purer light shall mark the road
　　That leads me to the Lamb.

'Walking with God' from *Olney Hymns* (1779), based on Genesis 5:24

79

Hark, my soul, it is the Lord;
'Tis thy Saviour, hear his word;
Jesus speaks, and speaks to thee:
'Say, poor sinner, lov'st thou me?

'I delivered thee when bound,
And when bleeding healed thy wound,
Sought thee wandering, set thee right,
Turned thy darkness into light.

'Can a woman's tender care
Cease towards the child she bare?
Yes, she may forgetful be,
Yet will I remember thee.

'Mine is an unchanging love,
Higher than the heights above,
Deeper than the depths beneath,
Free and faithful, strong as death.

'Thou shalt see my glory soon,
When the work of grace is done;
Partner of my throne shalt be;
Say, poor sinner, lov'st thou me?'

Lord, it is my chief complaint
That my love is cold and faint;
Yet I love thee and adore;
O for grace to love thee more!

From *Olney Hymns* (1779). Gladstone (q. v.) was so impressed with this
hymn that he translated it into Italian.

GEORGE CRABBE
(1754–1832) English poet

Crabbe was apprenticed at first to a doctor and later was a curate at his birthplace of Aldeburgh, Suffolk, before becoming chaplain to the Duke of Rutland. In 1814 he was appointed Vicar of Trowbridge. The favourite poet of Jane Austen, he was called 'the English Juvenal' by his friend Sir Walter Scott (q. v.).

80

>Pilgrim! burdened with thy sin,
>   Come the way to Zion's gate;
>There, till mercy speaks within,
>   Knock, and weep, and watch, and wait:
>Knock – He knows the sinner's cry;
>   Weep – He loves the mourner's tears;
>Watch – for saving grace is nigh;
>   Wait – till heavenly light appears.
>
>Hark it is the Bridegroom's voice,
>   'Welcome, pilgrim! to thy rest.'
>Now within the gate rejoice,
>   Safe, and sealed, and bought, and blest:
>Safe – from all the lures of vice;
>   Sealed – by signs the chosen know;
>Bought – by love and life the price;
>   Blest – the mighty debt to owe.
>
>Holy pilgrim! what for thee,
>   In a world like this remains?
>From thy guarded breast shall flee
>   Fear and shame, and doubt, and pain:
>Fear – the hope of heaven shall fly;
>   Shame – from glory's view retire;
>Doubt – in certain rapture die;
>   Pain – in endless bliss expire.

Fom 'Sir Eustace Grey' in *The Parish Register* (1807)

✤ ✤ ✤

RICHARD CRASHAW
(*c.* 1613–49) English poet

The religious poet Richard Crashaw was the son of a Puritan but converted to Catholicism and fled to Europe, where with the help of Charles I's exiled Catholic wife, Henrietta Maria, he worked for Cardinal Palotta in Italy and at the Santa Casa of Loreto.

81

Gloomy night embraced the place
    Wherein the noble Infant lay;
The Babe look'd up and shew'd His face,
    In spite of darkness it was day!
It was Thy day, Sweet! and did rise,
    Not from the east, but from Thine eyes.

Winter chid aloud, and sent
    The angry North to wage his wars.
The North forgot his fierce intent,
    And left perfumes instead of scars.
By those sweet eyes' persuasive powers
    Where he meant frost, he scattered flowers.

We saw Thee in Thy balmy nest,
    Young Dawn of our eternal day!
We saw Thine eyes break from their east
    And chase the trembling shades away,
We saw Thee; and we blessed the sight,
    We saw Thee by Thy Own sweet light.

Welcome, all wonders in one sight!
    Eternity shut in a span!
Summer in winter, day in night!
    Heaven in earth, and God in man!
Great little One! Whose lowly birth,
    Lifts earth to heav'n, stoops Heav'n to earth.

To Thee, meek Majesty! soft King
   Of simple graces and sweet loves;
Each one of us his lamb will bring,
   And each his pair of silver doves;
Till burnt in fire of Thy fair eyes,
   Ourselves become our sacrifice!

82

Lord, when the sense of thy sweet grace
Sends up my soul to seek thy face;
Thy blessèd eyes breed such desire,
I die in love's delicious fire.

O love, I am thy sacrifice.
Be still triumphant, blessèd eyes;
Still shine on me, fair suns! that I
Still may behold, though still I die.

Though still I die, I live again,
Still longing so to be still slain,
So gainful is such loss of breath;
I die e'en in desire of death.

Still live in me this loving strife
Of living death and dying life;
For while thou sweetly slayest me
Dead to myself, I live in thee.

83

Hear'st thou, my soul, what serious things
Both the Psalm and Sibyl sings
Of a sure Judge, from whose sharp ray
The world in flames shall fly away?

O that Trump, whose blast shall run
An even round with the circling sun,
And urge the murmuring graves to bring
Pale mankind forth to meet his King!

Dear Lord, remember in that day
Who was the cause thou cam'st this way!
Thy sheep was strayed, and thou would'st be
Even lost thyself in seeking me.

Shall all that labour, all that cost
Of love, and even that loss, be lost;
And this loved soul, judged worth no less
Than all that way and weariness?

Those mercies which thy Mary found,
And who thy Cross confessed and crowned,
Hope tells my heart, the same loves be
Still alive, and still for me.

Though both my prayers and tears combine,
Both worthless are, for they are mine;
But thou thy bounteous self still be,
And show thou art, by saving me.

ERASMUS DARWIN

(1731–1802) English botanist, poet and philosopher

The grandfather of both Charles Darwin and Francis Galton, Erasmus Darwin worked at first as a physician. The brother of the Rector of Elston, he lived in the Old Vicarage in Lichfield, Staffordshire, and was a close friend of the poet Anna Seward, daughter of the Prebendary of Lichfield who lived in the nearby Bishop's Palace. This hymn was written in 1795.

84

The Lord, how tender is his love!
   His justice how august!
Hence all her fears my soul derives;
   There anchors all her trust.

He showers the manna from above,
   To feed the barren waste;
Or points with death the fiery hail,
   And famine waits the blast.

He bids distress forget to groan,
   The sick from anguish cease;
In dungeons spreads his healing wing,
   And softly whispers peace.

For me, O Lord, whatever lot
   The hours commissioned bring;
Should all my withering blessing die,
   Or fairer clusters spring; –

O grant that still, with grateful heart,
   My years resigned may run,
'Tis thine to give, or to resume;
   And let thy will be done.

JOHN DONNE
(1573–1631) English poet and clergyman

A relative of Sir Thomas More, the metaphysical poet Donne was educated as a Catholic but became an Anglican at the age of nineteen. At first Secretary to Elizabeth I's Lord Chancellor, Lord Ellesmere, he later took Holy Orders and eventually became Dean of St Paul's Cathedral. (This hymn plays on the author's name, which he pronounced 'Dunn'.)

85

Wilt thou forgive that sin, where I begun,
   Which was my sin though it were done before?
Wilt thou forgive that sin, through which I run,
   And do run still, though still I do deplore?
When thou hast done, thou hast not done,
           For I have more.

Wilt thou forgive that sin which I have won,
    Others to sin, and made my sin their door?
Wilt thou forgive that sin which I did shun
    A year or two, but wallowed in a score?
When thou hast done, thou hast not done,
        For I have more.

I have a sin of fear, that when I've spun
    My last thread, I shall perish on the shore;
But swear by thyself, that at my death thy Son
    Shall shine, as he shines now and heretofore:
And, having done that, thou hast done:
        I fear no more.

From *Poems* (1633)

JOHN DRYDEN

(1631–1700) English poet and dramatist

John Dryden became Poet Laureate in 1670 but after the Restoration produced mainly plays. He became a Roman Catholic on the accession of James II. This hymn is a translation of the ninth-century Latin poem '*Veni, Creator Spiritus*' attributed to Charlemagne (q. v.).

86

Veni, Creator Spiritus

Creator Spirit! by whose aid
The world's foundations first were laid,
Come, visit every pious mind,
Come, pour thy joys on human kind;
From sin and sorrow set us free,
And make thy temples worthy thee.

O Source of uncreated light,
The Father's promised Paraclete,
Thrice holy Fount, thrice holy Fire,
Our hearts with heavenly love inspire;
Come, and thy sacred unction bring
To sanctify us while we sing.

Plenteous of grace, descend from high,
Rich in thy sevenfold energy;
Thou Strength of his almighty hand
Whose power does heaven and earth command,
Give us thyself, that we may see
The Father and the Son by thee.

Immortal honour, endless fame
Attend the Almighty Father's Name;
The Saviour Son be glorified,
Who for lost man's redemption died;
And equal adoration be,
Eternal Paraclete, to thee.

Adapted by John Wesley (q. v.) from Dryden's original in
Miscellaneous Poems (1693)

WILLIAM DUNBAR

(*c*.1465–*c*.1530) Scottish poet and diplomat

One of Scotland's earliest major poets, William Dunbar was at
first a Franciscan priest and later carried out diplomatic
missions for James IV who awarded him a royal pension.

87

Experience does me so inspire
Of this false failing world I tire,
That evermore flits like a vane
Which to consider is a pain.

And for my cures in sundry place
With help, Sir, of your noble grace,
My silly soul shall ne'er be slain
Nor for such sin to suffer pain.

The foremost hope yet that I have
In all this world, so God me save,
Is in your grace, both crop and grain,
Which is a lessening of my pain.

From *Of the Warldis Instabilitie* ('silly' here means 'simple')

88

Rorate caeli desuper!
   Heavens, distil your balmy show'rs,
For now is ris'n the bright day-star
   From the rose Mary, flow'r of flow'rs.
   The clear Sun, whom no cloud devours,
Surmounting Phoebus in the east,
   Is comen of his heav'nly tow'rs:
Et nobis Puer natus est.

Sinners, be glad and penance do,
   And thank your Maker heartfully;
For He that ye might not come to
   To you is comen full humbly,
   Your soul-es with his blood to buy,
And loose you of the fiend's arrest–
   And only of his own mercy:
Pro nobis Puer natus est.

Now spring up flowers from the root,
   Revert you upward nat'rally,
In honour of this blessèd fruit
   That rose up from the rose Mary;
   Lay out your leav-es lustily,
From dead take life now at the last,
   In worship of that Prince worthy,
Qui nobis Puer natus est.

Sing, heav'n imperial, most of height!
　　Regions of air make harmony!
All fish in flood and fowl of flight
　　Be mirthful and make melody!
All '*Gloria in excelsis*' cry!
Heav'n, earth and sea, man, bird and beast–
　　He that is crown'd above the sky,
　　Pro nobis Puer natus est.

From 'Ode on the Nativity' (the Latin reads: 'Drop dew, ye heavens,
from above' and 'For us a Child is born')

ELIZABETH I

(1533–1603) Queen of England

Queen Elizabeth was an accomplished poet and translator.
This hymn has been ascribed to her.

89

Christ was the Word who spake it:
He took the bread and brake it:
And what his word doth make it,
That I believe and take it.

RALPH WALDO EMERSON
(1803–82) American poet and essayist

Born the son of a Unitarian minister, Emerson studied theology at Harvard and was at first Pastor of the Second Church in Boston before resigning and visiting Europe where he met Coleridge (q. v.), Wordsworth (q. v.) and Carlyle (q. v.). He later returned to the USA and lectured on transcendentalism. Walt Whitman (q. v.) was one of his greatest disciples.

90

We love the venerable house
    Our fathers built to God;–
In heaven are kept their grateful vows,
    Their dust endears the sod.

Here holy thoughts a light have shed
    From many a radiant face,
And prayers of humble virtue made
    The perfume of the place.

And anxious hearts have pondered here
    The mystery of life,
And prayed the eternal Light to clear
    Their doubts, and aid their strife.

From humble tenements around
    Came up the pensive train,
And in the church a blessing found
    That filled their homes again;

For faith and peace and mighty love
    That from the Godhead flow,
Showed them the life of Heaven above
    Springs from the life below.

They live with God; their homes are dust;
    Yet here their children pray,
And in this fleeting lifetime trust
    To find the narrow way.

On him who by the altar stands,
    On him thy blessing fall,
Speak through his lips thy pure commands,
    Thou heart that lovest all.

Written in 1833 for Rev. Chandler Robbins, Emerson's successor as Minister of the Second (Unitarian) Church in Boston and sung in the church at his ordination.

91

Out from the heart of nature rolled
The burdens of the Bible old;
The litanies of nations came,
Like the volcano's tongue of flame,
Up from the burning core below,
The canticles of love and woe.

The word unto the prophet spoken
Was writ on tables yet unbroken;
Still floats upon the morning wind,
Still whispers to the willing mind:
One accent of the Holy Ghost
The heedless world hath never lost.

From 'The Problem' in *Poems* (1846)

PHINEAS FLETCHER

(1582–1650) English poet and clergyman

A cousin of the famous playwright John Fletcher, son of the poet Giles Fletcher and brother of the poet and priest Giles Fletcher the Younger, Phineas was himself Rector of Higay, Norfolk, and wrote Spenserian verse. Best known for *The Purple Island*, his anti-Catholic *The Locust of Apollyonists* is said to have influenced Milton (q. v.).

92

Drop, drop, slow tears,
   And bathe those beauteous feet,
Which brought from heaven
     The news and Prince of Peace.

Cease not, wet eyes,
   His mercies to entreat;
To cry for vengeance
   Sin doth never cease.

     In your deep floods
       Drown all my faults and fears;
     Nor let his eye
       See sin, but through my tears.

93

If God build not the house, and lay
   The groundwork sure, whoever build,
It cannot stand one stormy day;
   If God be not the city's shield,
If he be not their bars and wall,
   In vain the watch-tower, men and all.

Though then thou wak'st when others rest,
   Though rising thou prevent'st the sun,
Though with lean care thou daily feast,
   Thy labour's lost and thou undone;
But God his child will feed and keep,
   And draw the curtain to his sleep.

From *Piscatorie Eclogs* (1633). 'Prevent' here means 'go before'.

✣ ✣ ✣

ST FRANCIS OF ASSISI
(1182–1226) Italian friar

Born Giovanni Francesco Bernadone, St Francis began the Franciscan order in Assisi, Italy, after suffering a severe illness. Its teachings include a vow of poverty and the love of nature. This popular hymn from St Francis's 'The Canticle of the Sun' is by W. H. Draper. A more accurate translation by Matthew Arnold (q. v.), also sometimes sung, appears in the latter's essay 'Pagan and Medieval Religious Sentiment' in *Essays in Criticism* (1865).

94

All creatures of our God and King,
Lift up your voice and with us sing
    Alleluia, alleluia!
Thou burning sun with golden beam,
Thou silver moon with softer gleam,
    O praise him, O praise him,
    Alleluia, alleluia, alleluia!

Thou rushing wind that art so strong,
Ye clouds that sail in heaven along,
    O praise him, alleluia!
Thou rising morn, in praise rejoice,
Ye lights of evening, find a voice:
    O praise him, etc.

Thou flowing water, pure and clear,
Make music for thy Lord to hear,
    Alleluia, alleluia!
Thou fire so masterful and bright,
That givest man both warmth and light.
    O praise him, etc.

Dear mother earth, who day by day
Unfoldest blessings on our way,
    O praise him, alleluia!
The flowers and fruits that in thee grow,
Let them his glory also show:
    O praise him, etc.

And all ye men of tender heart,
Forgiving others, take your part,
    O sing ye alleluia!
Ye who long pain and sorrow bear,
Praise God and on him cast your care:
    O praise him, etc.

And thou, most kind and gentle death,
Waiting to hush our latest breath,
    O praise him, alleluia!
Thou leadest home the child of God,
And Christ our Lord the way hath trod:
    O praise him, etc.

Let all things their Creator bless,
And worship him in humbleness;
    O praise him, Alleluia!
Praise, praise the Father, praise the Son,
And praise the Spirit, Three in One:
    O praise him, etc.

ST FRANCIS XAVIER

(1506–52) Spanish missionary

Born at the castle of Xavier near Sanguesa, Spain, the son of the Privy Councillor to the King of Navarre, St Francis Xavier became a celebrated missionary and was also (with Loyola, q. v.) a founder of the Society of Jesus, or Jesuits.

95

O Deus ego amo Te

My God, I love thee: not because
    I hope for heaven thereby,
Nor yet because who love thee not
    Are lost eternally.

Nor with the hope of gaining aught,
    Nor seeking a reward:
But as thyself hast lovèd me,
    O ever-loving Lord.

Even so I love thee, and will love,
    And in thy praise will sing
Solely because thou art my God,
    And my eternal King.

Translated by Edward Caswall in his *Lyra Catholica* (1849)

GEORGE GASCOIGNE

(*c.* 1525–77) English poet, politician and soldier

The soldier poet and playwright George Gascoigne was a
relative of Chief Justice Sir Wiliam Gascoigne. He was MP
for Bedford and later served in Holland in the armies of the
Prince of Orange.

96

You that have spent the silent night,
In sleep and quiet rest,
And joy to see the cheerful light
That riseth in the East:
Now clear your voice, now cheer your heart,
Come help me now to sing:
Each willing soul come bear a part,
To praise the heavenly King.

And you whom care in prison keeps
Or sickness doth suppress,
Or secret sorrow breaks your sleeps
Or dolours do distress:
Yet bear a part in doleful wise,
Yea, think it good accord
And full and fitting sacrifice
Each soul to praise the Lord.

Yet as this deadly night did last
But for a little space,
And heavenly day, now night is past,
Doth show his pleasant face:
So must we hope to see God's face
At last in heaven on high,
When we have changed this mortal place
For immortality.

Unto which joy for to attain
God grant us all his grace,
And send us after worldly pain
In heaven to have a place;
Where we may still enjoy that light
Which never shall decay:
Lord, for thy mercy lend us might,
To see that joyful day.

From 'Good Morrow' in *The Posies of George Gascoigne* (1574)

97

When thou hast spent the ling'ring day
In pleasure and delight,
Or after toil and weary way
Dost seek to rest at night:

Unto thy pains or pleasures past,
Add this one labour yet,
Ere sleep close up thine eye too fast
Do not thy God forget.

But search within thy secret thought
What deeds did thee befall:
And if thou find amiss in aught,
To God for mercy call.

And think, how well so e'er it be
That thou hast spent the day,
It came of God, and not of thee,
So to direct thy way.

From 'Good Night' in *The Posies of George Gascoigne* (1574)

❖ ❖ ❖

WILLIAM GASKELL

(1805–84) English clergyman

Unitarian Minister at the Cross Street Chapel, Manchester,
and Professor of English History and Literature at Manchester
New College, William Gaskell also wrote a number of hymns.
His wife was the famous author of *Cranford* and other novels.

98

Though lowly here our lot may be,
    High work have we to do–
In faith and trust to follow him
    Whose lot was lowly too.

Our days of darkness we may bear,
    Strong in our Father's love;
We lean on his almighty arm,
    And fix our hopes above.

Our lives enriched with gentle thoughts
    And loving deeds may be,
As streams that still the nobler grow,
    The nearer to the sea.

To duty firm, to conscience true,
    However tried and pressed,
In God's clear sight high work we do,
    If we but do our best.

Thus may we make the lowliest lot
　　With rays of glory bright;
Thus may we turn a crown of thorns
　　Into a crown of light.

First published in E. Courtauld's *Psalms, Hymns and Anthems* (1860)

ST GERMANUS
(634–734) Greek clergyman

Bishop of Cyzicus, St Germanus eventually became Patriarch
of his birthplace, Constantinople, but was forced to resign
when he defended the use of icons in church aginst the will of
Emperor Leo the Isaurian.

99

A great and mighty wonder,
　　A full and blessed cure!
The Rose has come to blossom
　　Which shall for ay endure:
　　　　Repeat the hymn again!
　　　　'To God on high be glory,
　　And peace on earth to men.'

While thus they sing your Monarch,
　　Those bright angelic bands,
Rejoice, ye vales and mountains,
　　Ye oceans, clap your hands:
　　　　Repeat the hymn again! etc.

The Word has dwelt among us,
　　The true light from on high;
And cherubim sing anthems
　　To shepherds, from the sky:
　　Repeat the hymn again! etc.

Since all he comes to succour,
　　By all be he adored,
The infant born in Bethlem,
　　The Saviour and the Lord:
　　　　Repeat the hymn again! etc.

And idol forms shall perish
And error shall decay
And Christ shall wield his sceptre
Our Lord and God for ay:
　　Repeat the hymn again! etc.

Translated from the Greek by J.M. Neale

WILLIAM EWART GLADSTONE
(1809–98) English statesman

The son of Sir John Gladstone MP, Liberal Prime Minister W.E. Gladstone considered the Church as a career before entering politics and later wrote a number of books and essays, including *The State in its Relations with the Church* (1838).

100

O lead my blindness by the hand,
Lead me to thy familiar feast,
Not here or now to understand,
Yet even here and now to taste,
How the eternal Word of heaven
On earth in broken bread is given.

We, who this holy precinct round
In one adoring circle kneel,
May we in one intent be bound,
And one serene devotion feel;
And grow around thy sacred shrine
Like tendrils of the deathless vine.

We, who with one blest food are fed,
Into one body may we grow,
And one pure life from thee, the Head,
Informing all the members, flow;
One pulse be felt in every vein,
One law of pleasure and of pain.

SIDNEY GODOLPHIN

(1610–43) English poet and soldier

The Royalist poet and MP for Helston, Sidney Godophin, was the son of Sir William Godolphin and brother of Francis Godolphin to whom Hobbes dedicated *Leviathan*. He was killed during the Civil War.

101

Lord, when the wise men came from far,
Led to thy cradle by a star,
Shepherds with humble fearfulness
Walked safely, though their light was less.

Wise men in tracing Nature's laws
Ascend unto the highest cause:
Though wise men better know the way,
It seems no honest heart can stray.

And since no creature comprehends
The Cause of causes, End of ends,
He who himself vouchsafes to know
Best pleases his Creator so.

There is no merit in the wise
But love, the shepherds' sacrifice:
Wise men, all ways of knowledge past,
To the shepherds' wonder came at last.

ST GREGORY THE GREAT
(540–604) Italian pope

A former praetor of Rome, Gregory renounced his position to become a monk and was elected Pope Gregory I in 590. The famous incident when he said Anglo-Saxon boys for sale in the Roman slave-market were '*Non Angli sed angeli*' ('Not Angles but angels') led to his sending St Augustine to England. A prolific writer he also introduced Gregorian chant to the Western Church.

102
Nocte surgentes

Father, we praise thee, now the night is over;
Active and watchful, stand we all before thee;
Singing, we offer prayer and meditation:
    Thus we adore thee.

Monarch of all things, fit us for thy mansions;
Banish our weakness, health and wholeness sending;
Bring us to heaven, where thy saints united
    Joy without ending.

All-holy Father, Son, and equal Spirit,
Trinity blessèd; send us thy salvation;
Thine is the glory, gleaming and resounding
    Through all creation.

Cardinal Newman (q. v.) translated this hymn as
'Let us arise and watch by night'.

GUSTAVUS ADOLPHUS
(1594–1632) King of Sweden

The great Swedish king Gustavus II, known as Gustavus Adolphus, married the daughter of the Elector of Brandenburg and was killed in battle while helping the German Protestants in their struggle against the Catholic League.

103

Be not dismayed, thou little flock,
Although the foe's fierce battle-shock,
 Loud on all sides, assail thee.
Though o'er thy fall they laugh secure,
Their triumph cannot long endure:
 Let not thy courage fail thee.

Thy cause is God's: go at his call,
And to his hand commit thy all.
 Fear thou no ill impending.
His Gideon shall arise for thee,
God's word and people manfully,
 In God's own time, defending.

Our hope is sure in Jesus' might;
Against themselves the godless fight,
 Themselves, not us, distressing.
Shame and contempt their lot shall be;
God is with us, with him are we;
 To us belongs his blessing.

THOMAS HARDY
(1840–1928) English novelist and poet

The son of a stonemason, Hardy had once considered taking holy orders but instead worked as an ecclesiastical architect before becoming a full-time novelist and poet. He married Emma Gifford, sister-in-law of the Rector of St Juliot, Cornwall.

104

To thee whose eye all nature owns,
Who hurlest dynasts from their thrones
And liftest those of low estate,
We sing, with her men consecrate!

Yea, Great and Good, thee, thee, we hail,
Who shak'st the strong, who shield'st the frail,
Who hadst not shaped such souls as we
If tender mercy lacked in thee.

Though times be when the mortal moan
Seems unascending to thy throne;
Though seers do not as yet explain
Why suffering sobs to thee in vain;

We hold that thy unscanted scope
Affords a food for final hope,
That mild-eyed Prescience ponders nigh
Life's loom, to lull it by and by.

Therefore we quire to highest height
The Wellwiller, the kindly Might
That balances the Vast for weal,
That purges as by wounds to heal.

The systemed suns the skies enscroll
Obey thee in their rhythmic roll,
Ride radiantly at thy command,
Are darkened by thy master-hand.

And these pale panting multitudes
Seen surging here, their moils, their moods,
All shall fulfil their joy in thee,
In thee abide eternally.

Exultant adoration give
The Alone, through whom all living live,
The Alone, in whom all dying die,
Whose means the End shall justify!

From *The Dynasts* (1904–8)

REGINALD HEBER

(1783–1826) English clergyman and hymnwriter

Winner of the Newdigate Prize for Poetry while a student at
Brasenose College, Oxford, Heber was a Fellow of All Souls
before becoming Rector of the family living at Hodnet,
Shropshire, and was later Bishop of Calcutta.

105

Holy, Holy, Holy! Lord God Almighty!
    Early in the morning our song shall rise to thee:
Holy, Holy, Holy! merciful and mighty!
    God in Three Persons, blessèd Trinity!

Holy, Holy, Holy! all the saints adore thee,
    Casting down their golden crowns around the glassy sea,
Cherubim and Seraphim falling down before thee,
    Which wert, and art, and evermore shalt be.

Holy, Holy, Holy! though the darkness hide thee,
    Though the eye of sinful man thy glory may not see,
Only thou art holy; there is none beside thee,
    Perfect in power, in love, and purity.

Holy, Holy, Holy! Lord God Almighty!
   All thy works shall praise thy name in earth and sky and sea;
Holy, Holy, Holy! merciful and mighty!
   God in Three Persons, blessèd Trinity!

From *Hymns* (1827). 'Of hymns I like Heber's "Holy, Holy, Holy" better than
most; and it is in a fine metre too' (Alfred, Lord Tennyson, q. v.).

106

From Greenland's icy mountains,
   From India's coral strand,
Where Afric's sunny fountains
   Roll down their golden sand,
From many an ancient river,
   From many a palmy plain,
They call us to deliver
   Their land from error's chain.

Can we whose souls are lighted
   With wisdom from on high,
Can we to men benighted
   The lamp of life deny?
Salvation! Oh, salvation!
   The joyful sound proclaim,
Till each remotest nation
   Has learn'd Messiah's name.

What though the spicy breezes
   Blow soft o'er Ceylon's isle,
Though every prospect pleases
   And only man is vile;
In vain with lavish kindness
   The gifts of God are strown,
The heathen in his blindness
   Bows down to wood and stone.

Waft, waft, ye winds, His story,
   And you, ye waters, roll,
Till, like a sea of glory,
   It spreads from pole to pole;
Till o'er our ransom'd nature
   The Lamb for sinners slain,
Redeemer, King, Creator,
   In bliss returns to reign.

First published in *Evangelical Magazine* (July 1821). Lines 15–16
inspired the poem 'The 'Eathen' (1896) by Kipling (q. v.).

107

The Son of God goes forth to war,
  A kingly crown to gain;
His blood-red banner streams afar:
  Who follows in his train?

Who best can drink his cup of woe,
  Triumphant over pain,
Who patient bears his cross below,
  He follows in his train.

The Martyr first, whose eagle eye
  Could pierce beyond the grave;
Who saw his Master in the sky,
  And called on him to save.

Like him, with pardon on his tongue
  In midst of mortal pain,
He prayed for them that did the wrong:
  Who follows in his train?

A glorious band, the chosen few
  On whom the Spirit came,
Twelve valiant Saints, their hope they knew,
  And mocked the cross and flame.

They met the tyrant's brandish'd steel,
  The lion's gory mane,
They bowed their necks the death to feel:
  Who follows in their train?

A noble army, men and boys,
  The matron and the maid,
Around the Saviour's throne rejoice
  In robes of light arrayed.

They climbed the steep ascent of heaven
  Through peril, toil, and pain:
O God, to us may grace be given
  To follow in their train.

From *Hymns* (1827)

108

Brightest and best of the sons of the morning,
    Dawn on our darkness and lend us Thine aid;
Star of the east, the horizon adorning,
    Guide where our Infant Redeemer is laid.

Cold on His cradle the dew-drops are shining,
    Low lies His head with the beasts of the stall:
Angels adore Him in slumber reclining,
    Maker and Monarch and Saviour of all.

Say, shall we yield Him, in costly devotion,
    Odours of Edom and offerings divine?
Gems of the mountain and pearls of the ocean,
    Myrrh from the forest or gold from the mine.

Vainly we offer each ample oblation,
    Vainly with gifts would each favour secure;
Richer by far is the heart's adoration
    Dearer to God are the prayers of the poor.

Brightest and best of the sons of the morning,
    Dawn on our darkness and lend us thine aid;
Star of the east, the horizon adorning,
    Guide where our Infant Redeemer is laid.

Published in *Christian Observer* (November 1811), this was the first
hymn Heber ever wrote.

GEORGE HERBERT

(1593–1633) English poet, politician and clergyman

Younger brother of Lord Herbert of Cherbury, George Herbert's mother was the patron of John Donne (q. v.). Elected a Fellow and then Reader in Rhetoric at Trinity College, Cambridge, he was later MP for Montgomery before taking Holy Orders and becoming Rector of Bemerton, Wiltshire.

109

Let all the world in every corner sing,
    My God and King!
  The heavens are not too high,
  His praise may thither fly:
  The earth is not too low,
  His praises there may grow.
Let all the world in every corner sing,
    My God and King!

Let all the world in every corner sing,
    My God and King!
  The Church with psalms must shout,
  No door can keep them out;
  But above all the heart
  Must bear the longest part.
Let all the world in every corner sing,
    My God and King!

'Antiphon' in *The Temple* (1633)

110

King of Glory, King of Peace,
  I will love thee;
And, that love may never cease,
  I will move thee.

Thou hast granted my request,
  Thou hast heard me;
Thou didst note my working breast,
  Thou hast spared me.

Wherefore with my utmost art
   I will sing thee,
And the cream of all my heart
   I will bring thee.

Though my sins against me cried,
   Thou didst clear me,
And alone, when they replied,
   Thou didst hear me.

Sev'n whole days, not one in sev'n,
   I will praise thee;
In my heart, though not in heav'n,
   I can raise thee.

Thou grew'st soft and moist with tears,
   Thou relentedst:
And when Justice call'd for fears,
   Thou dissentedst.

Small it is, in this poor sort
   To enrol thee;
E'en eternity's too short
   To extol thee.

From *The Temple* (1633)

III

The God of love my Shepherd is,
   And he that doth me feed;
While he is mine and I am his,
   What can I want or need?

He leads me to the tender grass,
   Where I both feed and rest;
Then to the streams that gently pass:
   In both I have the best.

Or if I stray, he doth convert,
  And bring my mind in frame,
And all this not for my desert,
  But for his holy name.

Yea, in death's shady black abode
  Well may I walk, not fear;
For thou art with me, and thy rod
  To guide, thy staff to bear.

Surely thy sweet and wondrous love
  Shall measure all my days;
And, as it never shall remove,
  So neither shall my praise.

Based on Psalm 23, from *The Temple* (1633)

112

Sweet day, so cool, so calm, so bright,
  The bridal of the earth and sky,
The dew shall weep thy fall to-night;
  For thou must die.

Sweet rose, whose hue, angry and brave,
  Bids the rash gazer wipe his eye,
Thy root is ever in its grave,
  And thou must die.

Sweet spring, full of sweet days and roses,
  A box where sweets compacted lie,
My music shows you have your closes,
  And all must die.

Only a sweet and virtuous soul,
  Like seasoned timber, never gives;
But, though the whole world turn to coal,
  Then chiefly lives.

From *The Temple* (1633)

ROBERT HERRICK

(1592–1674 English poet and clergyman

Apprenticed to his uncle Sir William Herrick, a goldsmith and MP for Leicester, Robert Herrick took Holy Orders in 1623 and became Incumbent at Dean Priory, Devonshire. Swinburne (q. v.) greatly admired his poetry which included 'Gather ye rosebuds while ye may' and 'Cherry ripe'.

113

Down with the rosemary and bays,
    Down with the mistletoe;
Instead of holly, now upraise
    The greener box, for show.
Thus times and seasons oft do shift;
    Each thing his turn doth hold;
New thoughts and things do now succeed,
    As former things grow old.

The holly hitherto did sway:
    Let box now domineer.
Until the dancing Easter day,
    Or Easter's eve appear.
Thus times and seasons oft do shift, etc.

Then youthful box, which now hath grace,
    Your houses to renew,
Grown old, surrender must his place
    Unto the crispèd yew.
Thus times and seasons oft do shift, etc.

When yew is out, then birch comes in,
    And many flowers beside,
Both of a fresh and fragrant kin,
    To honour Whitsuntide.
Thus times and seasons oft do shift, etc.

> Green rushes then, and sweetest bents
>   With cooler oaken boughs,
> Come in for comely ornaments,
>   To readorn the house.
> *Thus times and seasons oft do shift, etc.*

From *Noble Numbers* (1647), Gustav Holst composed music
especially for this hymn

114

In this world, the Isle of Dreams,
While we sit by sorrow's streams,
Tears and terrors are our themes
                    Reciting:

There no monstrous fancies shall
Out of hell an horror call,
To create, or cause at all
                    Affrighting.

But when once from hence we fly,
More and more approaching nigh,
Unto young Eternity
                    Uniting:

There in calm and cooling sleep
We our eyes shall never steep;
But eternal watch shall keep,
                    Attending

In that whiter Island, where
Things are evermore sincere;
Candour here, and lustre there
                    Delighting:

Pleasures, such as shall pursue
Me immortalized, and you;
And fresh joys, as never to
                    Have ending.

115

> In the hour of my distress,
> When temptations me oppress,
> And when I my sins confess,
>   Sweet Spirit, comfort me.

> When I lie within my bed,
> Sick in heart, and sick in head,
> And with doubts discomforted,
>   Sweet Spirit, comfort me.

> When the house doth sigh and weep,
> And the world is drowned in sleep,
> Yet mine eyes the watch do keep,
>   Sweet Spirit, comfort me.

When, God knows, I'm tossed about,
Either with despair or doubt,
Yet, before the glass be out,
      Sweet Spirit, comfort me.

When the Judgement is revealed,
And that opened which was sealed,
Even to thee I have appealed
      Sweet Spirit, comfort me.

THOMAS HEYWOOD

(*c.* 1575–*c.* 1641) English dramatist and poet

The author of some 200 plays, most of which have been lost,
the Jacobean dramatist Thomas Heywood was also an actor
and poet. These verses were set to music by Gustav Holst.

116

I sought thee round about, O thou my God,
   To find thy abode;
I said unto the earth, 'Speak, art thou he?'
   She answered me
She was not; and I asked of creatures all
   In general
Contained therein: they with one voice proclaim
That none amongst them challenged such a name.

But now, my God, by thy illumining grace,
   Thy glorious face
So far forth as thou wilt discovered be,
   Methinks I see;
And though invisible and infinite
   To human sight,
Thou in thy Goodness, Beauty, Truth, appearest,
In which to our frail senses thou art nearest.

O make us apt to seek and quick to find,
   Thou God most kind;
Give us love, hope, and faith in thee to trust,
   Thou God most just;
Remit all our offences, we entreat,
   Most good, most great;
Grant that our willing though unworthy quest
May through thy grace admit us 'mongst the blest.

From *The Hierarchie of the Blessed Angells* (1635)

JAMES HOGG

(1770–1835) Scottish poet and novelist

Known as 'the Ettrick Shepherd' after the town of his birth in
Selkirkshire, Hogg was discovered by Sir Walter Scott (q. v.)
and became a friend of Wordsworth (q. v.) and other literary
figures. He was later on the editorial board of *Blackwood's
Magazine* and edited the poems of Burns (q. v.).

117

Blessed be thy name for ever,
Thou of life the guard and giver!
Thou canst guard the creatures sleeping,
Heal the heart long broke with weeping,
All the fury subject keep
Of boiling cloud and chafed deep:
We have seen thy wondrous might
Through the shadows of the night.

God of evening's yellow ray!
God of silver-dawning day,
That rises from the distant sea
Like breathings of eternity!
God of stillness and of motion, –
Of the rainbow and the ocean, –
Of the mountain, rock and river!
Blessed be thy name for ever!

Thou who slumberest not, nor sleepest!
Blest are they thou kindly keepest:
Thine the flaming sphere of light!
Thine the darkness of the night!
Thine are all the gems of even,
God of angels, God of heaven!
God of life that fadeth never!
Glory to thy name for ever!

From 'The Palmer's Morning Hymn' in *Mador of the Moor* (1816)

OLIVER WENDELL HOLMES
(1809–94) American poet, novelist and academic

Son of a minister in the First Congregational Church at
Cambridge, Massachusetts, Oliver Wendell Holmes was
Professor of Anatomy and Physiology at Harvard University
and one of the founders of *Atlantic Monthly*. He also wrote
novels and verse.

118

Our Father! while our hearts unlearn
    The creeds that wrong thy name,
Still let our hallowed altars burn
    With faith's undying flame.

Not by the lightning-gleams of wrath
    Our souls thy face shall see;
The star of love must light the path
    That leads to heaven and thee.

Help us to read our Master's will
    Through every darkening stain
That clouds his sacred image still,
    And see him once again,–

The brother Man, the pitying Friend,
    Who weeps for human woes,
Whose pleading words of pardon blend
    With cries of raging foes.

If mid the gathering storms of doubt
    Our hearts grow faint and cold,
The strength we cannot live without
    Thy love will not withhold.

Our prayers accept: our sins forgive;
    Our youthful zeal renew:
Shape for us holier lives to live,
    And nobler work to do.

From *Complete Poetical Works* (1895)

119

Lord of all being, throned afar,
Thy glory flames from sun and star;
Centre and soul of every sphere,
Yet to each loving heart how near!

Sun of our life, thy quickening ray
Sheds on our path the glow of day;
Star of our hope, thy softened light
Cheers the long watches of the night.

Our midnight is thy smile withdrawn,
Our noontide is thy gracious dawn,
Our rainbow arch thy mercy's sign;
All, save the clouds of sin, are thine.

Lord of all life, below, above,
Whose light is truth, whose warmth is love,
Before thy ever-blazing throne
We ask no lustre of our own.

Grant us thy truth to make us free,
And kindling hearts that burn for thee,
Till all thy living altars claim
One holy light, one heavenly flame.

From *The Professor at the Breakfast-Table* (1860)

120

Thou gracious God, whose mercy lends
The light of home, the smile of friends,
Our gathered flock thine arms enfold
As in the peaceful days of old.

Wilt thou not hear us while we raise
In sweet accord of solemn praise
The voices that have mingled long
In joyous flow of mirth and song?

For all the blessings life has brought,
For all its sorrowing hours have taught,
For all we mourn, for all we keep,
The hands we clasp, the loved that sleep,

The noon-tide sunshine of the past,
These brief, bright moments fading fast,
The stars that gild our darkening years,
The twilight ray from holier spheres,

We thank thee, Father; let thy grace
Our loving circle still embrace,
Thy mercy shed its heavenly store,
Thy peace be with us evermore.

121

O Lord of hosts, almighty King,
Behold the sacrifice we bring;
To every arm thy strength impart;
Thy Spirit shed through every heart.

Wake in our breasts the living fires,
The holy faith that warmed our sires:
Thy hand hath made our nation free;
To die for her is serving thee.

Be thou a pillared flame to show
The midnight snare, the silent foe;
And when the battle thunders loud,
Still guide us in its moving cloud.

God of all nations, sovereign Lord,
In thy dread name we draw the sword;
We lift the meteor flag on high,
That fills with light our troubled sky.

From treason's rent, from murder's stain
Guard thou its folds till peace shall reign
Till fort and field, till shore and sea,
Join our loud anthem, Praise to thee.

GERARD MANLEY HOPKINS

(1844–89) English poet and academic

Influenced by Newman (q. v.) and the Oxford Movement when
a student, Hopkins became a Catholic in 1866 and eventually
was appointed Professor of Greek and Latin at University
College, Dublin.

122

Godhead here in hiding, whom I do adore
Masked by these bare shadows, shape and nothing more,
See, Lord, at thy service low lies here a heart
Lost, all lost in wonder at the God thou art.

Seeing, touching, tasting are in thee deceived;
How says trusty hearing? that shall be believed;
What God's Son hath told me, take for truth I do;
Truth himself speaks truly, or there's nothing true.

On the Cross thy Godhead made no sign to men;
Here thy very manhood steals from human ken;
Both are my confession, both are my belief,
And I pray the prayer of the dying thief.

I am not like Thomas, wounds I cannot see,
But can plainly call thee Lord and God as he;
This faith each day deeper be my holding of,
Daily make me harder hope and dearer love.

O thou our reminder of Christ crucified,
Living Bread, the life of us for whom he died,
Lend this life to me then; feed and feast my mind,
There be thou the sweetness man was meant to find.

Jesu, whom I look at shrouded here below,
I beseech thee send me what I long for so,
Some day to gaze on thee face to face in light
And be blest for ever with thy glory's sight.

This is a translation of a hymn ascribed to St Thomas Aquinas (q. v.).

✛ ✛ ✛

THOMAS HUGHES

(1823–96) Lawyer, politican and novelist

A member of the Christian Socialist group which included Charles Kingsley (q. v.), Thomas Hughes was successively a QC and a County Court Judge and also served as a Liberal MP. His most famous book, *Tom Brown's Schooldays*, was first published anonymously. This was his only hymn.

123

O God of truth, whose living word
 Upholds whate'er hath breath,
Look down on thy creation, Lord,
 Enslaved by sin and death.

Set up thy standard, Lord, that we,
 Who claim a heavenly birth
May march with thee to smite the lies
 That vex thy groaning earth.

Ah! would we join that blest array
 And follow in the might
Of him, the faithful and the true,
 In raiment clean and white!

We fight for truth? we fight for God?
 Poor slaves of lies and sin!
He who would fight for thee on earth
 Must first be true within.

Then, God of truth, for whom we long,
 Thou who wilt hear our prayer,
Do thine own battle in our hearts
 And slay the falsehood there.

Yea, come! Then, tried as in the fire,
    From every lie set free,
Thy perfect truth shall dwell in us,
    And we shall live in thee.

First published in Mrs Norton's *The Lays of the Sanctuary* (1859)

POPE INNOCENT III
(1161–1216) Italian pope

Lotario de' Conti, who served as Pope Innocent III from 1198 until his death, was born in Agnagni, Italy. A very powerful pope, he attacked the Albigenses and excommunicated King John of England for refusing to recognise Stephen Langton as Archbishop of Canterbury.

124
Veni, Sancte Spiritus

Come, thou Holy Spirit, come;
And from thy celestial home
    Shed a ray of light divine;
Come, thou Father of the poor,
Come, thou Source of all our store,
    Come, within our bosoms shine:

Thou of comforters the best,
Thou the soul's most welcome Guest,
    Sweet refreshment here below;
In our labour rest most sweet,
Grateful coolness in the heat,
    Solace in the midst of woe.

O most blessèd Light divine,
Shine within these hearts of thine,
   And our inmost being fill;
Where thou art not, man hath nought,
Nothing good in deed or thought,
   Nothing free from taint of ill.

Heal our wounds; our strength renew;
On our dryness pour thy dew;
   Wash the stains of guilt away:
Bend the stubborn heart and will;
Melt the frozen, warm the chill;
   Guide the steps that go astray.

On the faithful, who adore
And confess thee, evermore
   In thy sevenfold gifts descend;
Give them virtue's sure reward,
Give them thy salvation, Lord,
   Give them joys that never end.

Translated by Edward Caswall in his *Lyra Catholica* (1849)

ST JOHN OF DAMASCUS

(d. *c.* 750) Greek theologian

St John Damascene was born in Damascus and became a monk at the monastery of St Sabas near Jerusalem. The last of the Greek Fathers, he is best known as a hymnwriter for his 'canons' (a canon was a series of odes, usually eight or nine in number, involving an acrostic).

125

The day of resurrection!
    Earth, tell it out abroad;
The passover of gladness,
    The passover of God!
From death to life eternal,
    From earth unto the sky,
Our Christ hath brought us over
    With hymns of victory.

Our hearts be pure from evil,
    That we may see aright
The Lord in rays eternal
    Of resurrection light;
And, listening to his accents,
    May hear, so calm and plain,
His own 'All hail!' and, hearing,
    May raise the victor strain.

Now let the heavens be joyful;
    Let earth her song begin;
Let the round world keep triumph,
    And all that is therein;
Let all things seen and unseen
    Their notes of gladness blend,
For Christ the Lord hath risen
    Our Joy that hath no end.

Translated by John Mason Neale in his
Hymns of the Eastern Church (1862)

126

Come, ye faithful, raise the strain
    Of triumphant gladness;
God hath brought his Israel
    Into joy from sadness;
Loosed from Pharaoh's bitter yoke
    Jacob's sons and daughters;
Led them with unmoistened foot
    Through the Red Sea waters.

'Tis the spring of souls today;
    Christ hath burst his prison,
And from three days' sleep in death
    As a sun hath risen:
All the winter of our sins,
    Long and dark, is flying
From his light, to whom we give
    Laud and praise undying.

Now the queen of seasons, bright
   With the day of splendour,
With the royal feast of feasts,
   Comes its joy to render;
Comes to gladden Christian men,
   Who with true affection
Welcome in unwearied strains
   Jesus' resurrection.

Neither might the gates of death,
   Nor the tomb's dark portal,
Nor the watchers, nor the seal,
   Hold thee as a mortal;
But arising thou dost stand
   'Midst thine own, bestowing
Thine own peace, which evermore
   Passeth human knowing.

Based on the Canticle of Moses in Exodus 15, this translation by J. M.
Neale first appeared in the *Christian Remembrancer* (April 1859)

DR SAMUEL JOHNSON

(1709–84) English lexicographer, critic and poet

This hymn by the celebrated Dr Johnson is a translation
from Boethius' most famous book *De Consolatione Philosophiae*.
Ancius Manlius Serinus Boethius (*c.* 475–524) was a Roman
statesman serving under Theodoric during the Gothic
occupation of the city.

127

O thou whose power o'er moving worlds presides,
Whose voice created, and whose wisdom guides,
On darkling man in pure effulgence shine,
And cheer the clouded mind with light divine.

'Tis thine alone to calm the pious breast
With silent confidence and holy rest:
From thee, great God, we spring, to thee we tend, –
Path, Motive, Guide, Original, and End.

BEN JONSON

(1573–1637) English dramatist, actor and poet

Ben Jonson was born in London, the posthumous son of a clergyman. After killing a fellow actor in a brawl he escaped hanging by benefit of clergy and became a Catholic while in prison but later returned to Anglicanism. As well as plays and poetry he also produced court masques during the reign of King James I.

128

I sing the birth was born tonight,
The author both of life and light,
    The angels so did sound it;
And like the ravished shepherds said,
Who saw the light, and were afraid,
    Yet searched, and true they found it.

The Son of God, the Eternal King,
That did us all salvation bring,
    And freed our soul from danger,
He whom the whole world could not take,
The Word, which heaven and earth did make,
    Was now laid in a manger.

The Father's wisdom willed it so,
The Sun's obedience knew no No,
    Both wills were in one stature,
And, as that wisdom had decreed,
The Word was now made flesh indeed,
    And took on him our nature.

What comfort by him do we win,
Who made himself the price of sin,
    To make us heirs of glory!
To see this Babe, all innocence,
A martyr born in our defence,
    Can man forget the story?

'A Hymn on the Nativity of My Saviour' from *Works* (1640)

✣ ✣ ✣

ST JOSEPH THE HYMNOGRAPHER

(*c*. 800–83) Sicilian monk

After a period in Thessalonica and Constantinople, St Joseph
was captured by pirates and served as a slave in Crete. He later
established a monastery in Constantinople and was made
keeper of the sacred vessels of the Great Church in the city by
Empress Theodora.

129

Stars of the morning, so gloriously bright,
Filled with celestial resplendence and light,
These that, where night never followeth day,
Raise the Trisagion ever and aye:

These are thy counsellors, these dost thou own,
Lord God of Sabaoth, nearest thy throne;
These are thy ministers, these dost thou send,
Help of the helpless ones, man to defend.

These keep the guard amid Salem's dear bowers;
Thrones, Principalities, Virtues, and Powers;
Where, with the Living Ones, mystical Four,
Cherubim, Seraphim bow and adore.

'Who like the Lord?' thunders Michael the Chief;
Raphael, 'the cure of God', comforteth grief;
And, as at Nazareth, prophet of peace,
Gabriel, the 'Light of God', bringeth release.

Then, when the earth was first poised in mid space,
Then, when the planets first sped on their race,
Then, when were ended the six days employ,
Then all the Sons of God shouted for joy.

Still let them succour us; still let them fight,
Lord of angelic hosts, battling for right;
Till, where their anthems they ceaselessly pour,
We with the angels may bow and adore.

Translated by J. M. Neale in his *Hymns of the Eastern Church* (1862)

130

Let us now our voices raise,
 Wake the day with gladness:
God himself to joy and praise
 Turns our human sadness;
Joy that martyrs won their crown,
 Opened heaven's bright portal,
When they laid the mortal down
 For the life immortal.

Never flinched they from the flame,
 From the torment never;
Vain the tyrant's sharpest aim,
 Vain each fierce endeavour:
For by faith they saw the land
 Decked in all its glory,
Where triumphant now they stand
 With the victor's story.

Up and follow, Christian men!
 Press through toil and sorrow;
Spurn the night of fear, and then,
 O the glorious morrow!
Who will venture on the strife?
 Who will first begin it?
Who will grasp the Land of Life?
 Warriors, up and win it!

   Translated by J. M. Neale in his
   Hymns of the Eastern Church (1862)

JOHN KEBLE

(1792–1866) English clergyman, poet and scholar

The son of the Vicar of Coln St Oldwyn, Gloucestershire, Keble was elected a Fellow of Oriel College, Oxford, aged nineteen. He was later ordained deacon and after publication of his famous book of poetry *The Christian Year* (1827) became Professor of Poetry at Oxford University (1831). With Newman (q. v.) and Pusey he began the Oxford Movement, or Tractarians.

131

Bless'd are the pure in heart,
For they shall see our God,
The secret of the Lord is theirs,
Their soul is Christ's abode.

Still to the lowly soul
He doth himself impart,
And for his dwelling and his throne
Chooseth the pure in heart.

The Lord, who left the heavens
Our life and peace to bring,
To dwell in lowliness with men,
Their Pattern and their King;

Lord, we thy presence seek;
May ours this blessing be;
Give us a pure and lowly heart
A temple meet for thee.

From 'The Purification' in *The Christian Year* (1827)

132

When God of old came down from heaven
    In power and wrath he came;
Before his feet the clouds were riven,
    Half darkness and half flame.

But when he came the second time,
    He came in power and love;
Softer than gale at morning prime
    Hovered his holy Dove.

The fires, that rushed on Sinai down
    In sudden torrents dread,
Now gently light, a glorious crown,
    On every sainted head.

And as on Israel's awe-struck ear
　　The voice exceeding loud,
The trump that angels quake to hear,
　　Thrilled from the deep dark cloud:

So, when the Spirit of our God
　　Came down his flock to find,
A Voice from heaven was heard abroad,
　　A rushing, mighty Wind.

It fills the Church of God; it fills
　　The sinful world around:
Only in stubborn hearts and wills
　　No place for it is found.

Come, Lord, come Wisdom, Love, and Power,
　　Open our ears to hear;
Let us not miss the accepted hour;
　　Save, Lord, by love or fear.

From *The Christian Year* (1827)

133

There is a book, who runs may read,
　　Which heavenly truth imparts,
And all the lore its scholars need,
　　Pure eyes and Christian hearts.
The works of God above, below,
　　Within us and around,
Are pages in that book, to show
　　How God himself is found.

The glorious sky, embracing all,
　　Is like the Maker's love,
Wherewith encompassed, great and small
　　In peace and order move.
The moon above, the Church below,
　　A wondrous race they run;
But all their radiance, all their glow,
　　Each borrows of its sun.

The Saviour lends the light and heat
    That crown his holy hill;
The saints, like stars, around his seat
    Perform their courses still.
The dew of heaven is like thy grace,
    It steals in silence down;
But where it lights, the favoured place
    By richest fruits is known.

One name, above all glorious names,
    With its ten thousand tongues
The everlasting sea proclaims,
    Echoing angelic songs.
The raging fire, the roaring wind,
    Thy boundless power display;
But in the gentler breeze we find
    Thy Spirit's viewless way.

Two worlds are ours: 'tis only sin
    Forbids us to descry
The mystic heaven and earth within,
    Plain as the sea and sky.
Thou who hast given me eyes to see
    And love this sight so fair,
Give me a heart to find out thee,
    And read thee everywhere.

From *The Christian Year* (1827)

134

New every morning is the love
Our wakening and uprising prove;
Through sleep and darkness safely brought,
Restored to life, and power, and thought.

New mercies, each returning day,
Hover around us while we pray;
New perils past, new sins forgiven,
New thoughts of God, new hopes of heaven.

If on our daily course our mind
Be set to hallow all we find,
New treasures still, of countless price,
God will provide for sacrifice.

Old friends, old scenes, will lovelier be,
As more of heaven in each we see;
Some softening gleam of love and prayer
Shall dawn on every cross and care.

We need not bid, for cloistered cell,
Our neighbour and our work farewell,
Nor strive to wind ourselves too high
For sinful man beneath the sky.

The trivial round, the common task,
Would furnish all we ought to ask,–
Room to deny ourselves, a road
To bring us daily nearer God.

Only, O Lord, in thy dear love
Fit us for perfect rest above;
And help us this and every day
To live more nearly as we pray.

From *The Christian Year* (1827)

THOMAS KEN

(1637–1711) English clergyman

Thomas Ken was brought up by Isaak Walton, who was married to his eldest sister Ann. Elected a Fellow of New College, Oxford, in 1657, he was Chaplain to the wife of William of Orange in Holland, Chaplain to Charles II and later Bishop of Bath and Wells. One of the seven bishops sent to the Tower by James II for refusing to read the Declaration of Indulgence, he lost his bishopric by refusing to take the oath to William when crowned King of England but was later granted a pension by Queen Anne.

135

Awake, my soul, and with the sun
Thy daily stage of duty run,
Shake off dull sloth, and joyful rise
To pay thy morning sacrifice.

Thy precious time misspent, redeem,
Each present day thy last esteem,
Improve thy talent with due care,
For the Great Day thyself prepare.

By influence of the Light divine
Let thy own light to others shine.
Reflect all heaven's propitious ways
In ardent love, and cheerful praise.

Wake, and lift up thyself, my heart,
And with the angels bear thy part,
Who all night long unwearied sing
High praise to the eternal King.

All praise to thee who safe hast kept
And hast refreshed me while I slept.
Grant, Lord, when I from death shall wake
I may of endless light partake.

Heav'n is, dear Lord, where e'er thou art,
O never then from me depart;
For to my soul 'tis hell to be
But for one moment void of thee.

Lord, I my vows to thee renew,
Disperse my sins like morning dew.
Guard my first springs of thought and will
And with thyself my Spirit fill.

Direct, control, suggest this day
All I design, or do, or say,
That all my powers with all their might
In thy sole glory may unite.

Praise God, from whom all blessings flow,
Praise him, all creatures here below,
Praise him above, ye heavenly host,
Praise Father, Son, and Holy Ghost.

From *Manual of Prayers* (1674)

136

Glory to thee, my God, this night
For all the blessings of the light;
Keep me, O keep me, King of Kings,
Beneath thine own almighty wings.

Forgive me, Lord, for thy dear Son,
The ill that I this day have done;
That with the world, myself, and thee,
I, ere I sleep, at peace may be.

Teach me to live, that I may dread
The grave as little as my bed;
Teach me to die, that so I may
Rise glorious at the awful day.

O may my soul on thee repose,
And may sweet sleep mine eyelids close,
Sleep that shall me more vigorous make
To serve my God when I awake.

If in the night I sleepless lie,
My soul with heavenly thoughts supply;
Let no ill dreams disturb my rest,
No powers of darkness me molest.

Praise God, from whom all blessings flow;
Praise him, all creatures here below;
Praise him above, ye heavenly host;
Praise Father, Son, and Holy Ghost.

From *Manual of Prayers* (1674)

CHARLES KINGSLEY

(1819–75) English writer and clergyman

Best known as the author of *The Water Babies* and *Westward Ho!* and other books, Charles Kingsley was the son of a Devonshire vicar who became Rector of St Luke's, Chelsea. Kingsley himself was Rector of Eversley, Hampshire, and later became Chaplain to Queen Victoria (1859), Professor of Modern History at Cambridge University and a canon of Westminster Abbey. Anti-Tractarian, he was a founder of the Christian Socialist Movement.

137

From thee all skill and science flow,
All pity, care, and love,
All calm and courage, faith and hope:
O pour them from above!

And part them, Lord, to each and all,
    As each and all shall need
To rise, like incense, each to thee,
    In noble thought and deed.

And hasten, Lord, that perfect day
    When pain and death shall cease,
And thy just rule shall fill the earth
    With health, and light, and peace;

When ever blue the sky shall gleam,
    And ever green the sod,
And man's rude work deface no more
    The paradise of God.

138

The day of the Lord is at hand, at hand;
    Its storms roll up the sky;
The nations sleep starving on heaps of gold;
    All dreamers toss and sigh;
The night is darkest before the morn;
When the pain is sorest the child is born,
    And the day of the Lord at hand.

Gather you, gather you, angels of God—
    Freedom and mercy and truth;
Come! for the earth is grown coward and old,
    Come down, and renew us her youth.
Wisdom, self-sacrifice, daring, and love,
Haste to the battle-field, stoop from above
    To the day of the Lord at hand.

Gather you, gather you, hounds of hell—
    Famine, and plague, and war;
Idleness, bigotry, cant, and misrule,
    Gather, and fall in the snare!
Hireling and Mammonite, bigot and knave,
Crawl to the battle-field, sneak to your grave,
    In the day of the Lord at hand.

Who would sit down and sigh for a lost age of gold,
   While the Lord of all ages is here?
True hearts will leap at the trumpet of God,
   And those who can suffer can dare.
Each old age of gold was an iron age too,
And the meekest of saints may find stern work to do
   In the day of the Lord at hand.

From *Andromeda and Other Poems* (1858)

HENRY WADSWORTH LONGFELLOW
(1807–82) American poet

The older brother of the Rev. Samuel Longfellow (q. v.), H. W.
Longfellow is famous for his long poem *The Song of Hiawatha*
(1858). Though he never claimed to be a hymnwriter, a
number of his poems have been used as hymns.

139

Tell me not, in mournful numbers,
   Life is but an empty dream!–
For the soul is dead that slumbers,
   And things are not what they seem.

Life is real! Life is earnest!
   And the grave is not its goal;
Dust thou art, to dust returnest,
   Was not spoken of the soul.

Not enjoyment, and not sorrow,
   Is our destined end or way;
But to act, that each to-morrow
   Find us farther than to-day.

Art is long, and Time is fleeting,
   And our hearts, though stout and brave,
Still, like muffled drums, are beating
   Funeral marches to the grave.

In the world's broad field of battle,
    In the bivouac of Life,
Be not like dumb, driven cattle!
    Be a hero in the strife!

Trust no Future, howe'er pleasant!
    Let the dead Past bury its dead!
Act, – act in the living Present!
    Heart within, and God o'erhead!

Lives of great men all remind us
    We can make our lives sublime,
And, departing, leave behind us
    Footprints on the sands of time;

Footprints, that perhaps another,
    Sailing o'er life's solemn main,
A forlorn and shipwrecked brother,
    Seeing, shall take heart again.

Let us, then, be up and doing,
    With a heart for any fate;
Still achieving, still pursuing,
    Learn to labor and to wait.

'A Psalm of Life' from *Voices in the Night* (1839)

140

Down the dark future, through long generations,
    The sounds of war grow fainter and then cease;
And, like a bell with solemn sweet vibrations,
    I hear once more the voice of Christ say 'Peace'!

Peace! and no longer, from its brazen portals,
    The blast of war's great organ shakes the skies;
But beautiful as songs of the immortals,
    The holy melodies of love arise.

From 'The Arsenal at Springfield' in *The Belfry of Bruges* (1845)

141

All is of God! If he but wave his hand
   The mists collect, the rain falls thick and loud,
Till, with a smile of light on sea and land,
   Lo! he looks back from the departing cloud.

Angels of Life and Death alike are his;
   Without his leave they pass no threshold o'er;
Who, then, would wish or dare, believing this,
   Against his messengers to shut the door?

From 'The Two Angels' in *Birds of Passage* (1858)

142

The Saviour said: 'Yet one thing more;
   If thou wouldst perfect be,
Sell all thou hast and give it to the poor,
   And come and follow me!'

Within this temple Christ again, unseen,
   Those sacred words hath said
And his invisible hands to-day have been
   Laid on a young man's head.

And evermore beside him on his way
   The unseen Christ shall move,
That he may lean upon his arm and say,
   'Dost thou, dear Lord, approve?'

Beside him at the marriage feast shall be,
   To make the scene more fair;
Beside him in the dark Gethsemane
   Of pain and midnight prayer.

O holy trust! O endless sense of rest!
  Like the beloved John
To lay his head upon the Saviour's breast,
  And thus to journey on!

'Hymn for my Brother's Ordination' in *Seaside and Fireside* (1851). This
version (the original begins 'Christ to the Young Man Said') is from
the *Plymouth Collection* (1855) by Rev. Henry Ward Beecher, brother of
Harriet Beecher Stowe (q. v.).

SAMUEL LONGFELLOW

(1819–92) American clergyman

The younger brother of the poet Henry Wadsworth Longfellow
(q. v.), whose biography he wrote, Samuel Longfellow was a
Unitarian minister in Massachusetts, Brooklyn and
Pennsylvania.

143

Holy Spirit, Truth Divine,
Dawn upon this soul of mine;
Word of God, and inward Light,
Wake my spirit; clear my sight.

Holy Spirit, Love Divine,
Glow within this heart of mine;
Kindle every high desire;
Perish self in thy pure fire.

Holy Spirit, Power Divine,
Fill and nerve this will of mine;
By thee may I strongly live,
Bravely bear, and nobly strive.

Holy Spirit, Right Divine,
King within my conscience reign;
Be my law, and I shall be
Firmly bound, for ever free.

Holy Spirit, Peace Divine,
Still this restless heart of mine;
Speak to calm this tossing sea,
Stayed in thy tranquillity.

Holy Spirit, Joy Divine,
Gladden thou this heart of mine;
In the desert ways I sing,
'Spring, O Well, for ever spring!'

From Samuel Johnson and Samuel Longfellow, *Hymns of the Spirit* (1864)

144

'Tis winter now; the fallen snow
    Has left the heavens all coldly clear;
Through leafless boughs the sharp winds blow,
    And all the earth lies dead and drear.

And yet God's love is not withdrawn;
    His life within the keen air breathes;
His beauty paints the crimson dawn,
    And clothes the boughs with glittering wreaths.

And though abroad the sharp winds blow,
    And skies are chill, and frosts are keen,
Home closer draws her circle now,
    And warmer glows her light within.

O God! who giv'st the winter's cold,
    As well as summer's joyous rays,
Us warmly in thy love enfold,
    And keep us through life's wintry days.

From Samuel Johnson and Samuel Longfellow, *Hymns of the Spirit* (1864)

145

The summer days are come again;
    Once more the glad earth yields
Her golden wealth of ripening grain,
    And breath of clover fields,
And deepening shade of summer woods,
    And glow of summer air,
And winging thoughts, and happy moods
    Of love and joy and prayer.

The summer days are come again;
    The birds are on the wing;
God's praises, in their loving strain,
    Unconsciously they sing.
We know who giveth all the good
    That doth our cup o'erbrim;
For summer joy in field and wood
    We lift our song to him.

146

Again, as evening's shadow falls,
We gather in these hallowed walls;
And vesper hymn and vesper prayer
Rise mingling on the holy air.

May struggling hearts, that seek release,
Here find the rest of God's own peace;
And strengthened here by hymn and prayer
Lay down the burden and the care.

O God our light, to thee we bow:
Within all shadows standest thou:
Give deeper calm than night can bring:
Give sweeter songs than lips can sing.

Life's tumult we must meet again,
We cannot at the shrine remain:
But in the spirit's secret cell
May hymn and prayer for ever dwell.

From *Vespers* (1859)

JAMES RUSSELL LOWELL

(1819–91) American poet, essayist and diplomat

The son of a minister, Lowell became Professor of Modern Languages and Literature at Harvard University (succeeding H. W. Longfellow, q. v.) and editor of *Atlantic Monthly*. As a diplomat he worked for the US Government in Spain and the UK. Though he wrote no hymns some of his poems have been used as such.

147

Once to every man and nation
    Comes the moment to decide,
In the strife of truth with falsehood,
    For the good or evil side:
Some great cause, God's new Messiah,
    Offering each the bloom or blight;
And the choice goes by for ever
    'Twixt that darkness and that light.

Then to side with truth is noble,
    When we share her wretched crust,
Ere her cause bring fame and profit,
    And 'tis prosperous to be just;
Then it is the brave man chooses,
    While the coward stands aside,
Till the multitude make virtue
    Of the faith they had denied.

By the light of burning martyrs,
    Christ, thy bleeding feet we track,
Toiling up new Calvaries ever
    With the cross that turns not back.
New occasions teach new duties;
    Time makes ancient good uncouth;
They must upward still and onward
    Who would keep abreast of truth.

Though the cause of evil prosper,
  Yet 'tis truth alone is strong;
Though her portion be the scaffold,
  And upon the throne be wrong,
Yet that scaffold sways the future,
  And, behind the dim unknown,
Standeth God within the shadow,
  Keeping watch above his own.

From 'The Present Crisis' in *Poems* (1849).
The crisis was the war between
the USA and Mexico.

148

Men, whose boast it is that ye
Come of fathers brave and free,
If there breathe on earth a slave,
Are ye truly free and brave?
If ye do not feel the chain
When it works a brother's pain,
Are ye not base slaves indeed,
Slaves unworthy to be freed?

Is true freedom but to break
Fetters for our own dear sake,
And, with leathern hearts, forget
That we owe mankind a debt?
No! true freedom is to share
All the chains our brothers wear,
And, with heart and hand, to be
Earnest to make others free.

They are slaves who fear to speak
For the fallen and the weak;
They are slaves who will not choose
Hatred, scoffing, and abuse,
Rather than in silence shrink
From the truth they needs must think;
They are slaves who dare not be
In the right with two or three.

From *Poems* (1844)

ST IGNATIUS LOYOLA

(1491–1556) Spanish soldier and ecclesiastic

Born in the Basque province of Guipuzcoa, Spain, Inigo
Lopez de Recalde served as a soldier before becoming a
pilgrim and then co-founder, with St Francis Xavier (q. v.), of
the Society of Jesus, or Jesuits, in 1534.

149

O Deus, ego amo te

Do I not love thee, Lord most high,
In answer to thy love for me?
I seek no other liberty
But that of being bound to thee.

May memory no thought suggest
But shall to thy pure glory tend;
My understanding find no rest
Except in thee, its only end.

My God, I here protest to thee,
No other will I have than thine;
Whatever thou hast given me
I here again to thee resign.

All mine is thine; say but the word,
Whate'er thou willest, – be it done:
I know thy love, all-gracious Lord;
I know it seeks my good alone.

Apart from thee all things are nought:
Then grant, O my supremest bliss!
Grant me to love thee as I ought:–
Thou givest all in giving this!

This translation is by Edward Caswall (1858) and appears in *Hymns for
the Christian Church and Home* compiled by James Martineau (q. v.)

MARTIN LUTHER

(1483–1546) German clergyman

The most important force in the Reformation, Martin Luther
was ordained priest in 1507. After a visit to Rome he attacked
corruption in the Church and the Pope's right to forgive sins,
refusing to retract his views when summoned before the Diet at
Worms (1521). He later translated the Scriptures into German
and married a former nun.

150

Ein' feste Burg ist unser Gott

A safe stronghold our God is still,
        A trusty shield and weapon;
He'll help us clear from all the ill
        That hath us now o'ertaken.
            The ancient prince of hell
            Hath risen with purpose fell;
            Strong mail of craft and power
            He weareth in this hour;
        On earth is not his fellow.

With force of arms we nothing can,
  Full soon were we down-ridden;
But for us fights the proper Man,
  Whom God himself hath bidden.
    Ask ye, Who is this same?
    Christ Jesus is his name,
    The Lord Sabaoth's Son;
    He, and no other one,
  Shall conquer in the battle.

And were this world all devils o'er,
  And watching to devour us,
We lay it not to heart so sore;
  Not they can overpower us.
    And let the prince of ill
    Look grim as e'er he will,
    He harms us not a whit;
    For why? – his doom is writ;
  A word shall quickly slay him.

God's word, for all their craft and force,
  One moment will not linger;
But, spite of hell, shall have its course;
  'Tis written by his finger.
    And though they take our life,
    Goods, honour, children, wife,
    Yet is their profit small;
    These things shall vanish all:
  The City of God remaineth!

Written for the Diet at Worms, Heine called this hymn 'The
Marseillaise of the Reformation'. This famous translation by Thomas
Carlyle (q. v.) appeared in *Fraser's Magazine* (1831).

151
Christ lag in Todesbanden

Christ Jesus lay in death's strong bands
　　For our offences given,
But now at God's right hand he stands
　　And brings us life from heaven:
　　Wherefore let us joyful be,
And sing to God right thankfully
　　Loud songs of Alleluia!
　　　Alleluia!

It was a strange and dreadful strife
　　When life and death contended;
The victory remained with life,
　　The reign of death was ended:
　　Stripped of power, no more he reigns,
An empty form alone remains;
　　His sting is lost for ever.

So let us keep the festival
　　Whereto the Lord invites us;
Christ is himself the joy of all,
　　The sun that warms and lights us;
　　By his grace he doth impart
Eternal sunshine to the heart;
　　The night of sin is ended.

Then let us feast this Easter day
　　On the true Bread of heaven.
The word of grace hath purged away
　　The old and wicked leaven;
　　Christ alone our soul will feed,
He is our meat and drink indeed,
　　Faith lives upon no other.

Translated by Richard Massie in Martin Luther's
Spiritual Songs (1854)

152

Von Himmel hoch da komm ich her

Give heed, my heart, lift up thine eyes:
Who is it in yon manger lies?
Who is this child so young and fair?
The blessèd Christ-child lieth there.

Welcome to earth, thou noble Guest,
Through whom even wicked men are blest!
Thou com'st to share our misery;
What can we render, Lord, to thee?

Were earth a thousand times as fair,
Beset with gold and jewels rare,
She yet were far too poor to be
A narrow cradle, Lord, for thee.

Ah! dearest Jesus, Holy Child,
Make thee a bed, soft, undefiled,
Within my heart, that it may be
A quiet chamber kept for thee.

My heart for very joy doth leap;
My lips no more can silence keep;
I too must raise with joyful tongue
That sweetest ancient cradle song.

'Glory to God in highest heaven,
Who unto man his Son hath given!'
While angels sing with pious mirth
A glad New Year to all the earth.

Translated by Catherine Winkworth in her
Lyra Germanica (1855)

HENRY FRANCIS LYTE

(1793–1847) Scottish poet, hymnwriter and clergyman

Born near Kelso, Lyte took Holy Orders in 1815 and was Perpetual Curate for nearly twenty-five years at Lower Brixham, Devon. His most famous hymn, 'Abide With Me', was sung by Nurse Edith Cavell on the night before her execution by the Germans in 1915.

153

Abide with me: fast falls the eventide;
The darkness deepens; Lord, with me abide:
When other helpers fail, and comforts flee,
Help of the helpless, O abide with me.

Swift to its close ebbs out life's little day;
Earth's joys grow dim, its glories pass away;
Change and decay in all around I see;
O thou who changest not, abide with me.

Not a brief glance I beg, a passing word;
But as thou dwellst with thy disciples, Lord,
Familiar, condescending, patient, free,
Come not to sojourn, but abide with me.

Come not in terrors as the King of Kings,
But kind and good, with healing in thy wings,
Tears for all woes, a heart for every plea–
Come, Friend of sinners, and thus bide with me.

Thou on my head in early youth didst smile;
And, though rebellious and perverse meanwhile,
Thou hast not left me, oft as I left thee,
On to the close, O Lord, abide with me!

I need thy presence every passing hour;
What but thy grace can foil the tempter's power?
Who like thyself my guide and stay can be?
Through cloud and sunshine, O abide with me.

I fear no foe with thee at hand to bless:
Ills have no weight, and tears no bitterness.
Where is death's sting? where grave thy victory?
I triumph still if thou abide with me.

Hold thou thy Cross before my closing eyes;
Shine through the gloom, and point me to the skies:
Heaven's morning breaks, and earth's vain shadows flee;
In life, in death, O Lord, abide with me.

From *Remains* (1850)

154

Praise, my soul, the King of heaven!
    To his feet thy tribute bring.
Ransomed, healed, restored, forgiven,
    Who like me his praise should sing?
        Praise him! Praise him!
    Praise the everlasting King!

Praise him for his grace and favour
    To our fathers in distress;
Praise him still the same for ever,
    Slow to chide, and swift to bless.
        Praise him! Praise him!
    Glorious in his faithfulness.

Father-like, he tends and spares us;
    Well our feeble frame he knows;
In his hands he gently bears us,
    Rescues us from all our foes.
        Praise him! Praise him!
    Widely as his mercy flows.

Frail as summer's flower we flourish:
    Blows the wind, and it is gone.
But, while mortals rise and perish,
    God endures unchanging on.
        Praise him! Praise him!
    Praise the high eternal One!

Angels, help us to adore him:
　　Ye behold him face to face;
Sun and moon, bow down before him,
　　Dwellers all in time and space.
　　　　Praise him! Praise him!
　　Praise with us the God of grace!

Based on Psalm 103, from *Spirit of the Psalms* (1834)

GEORGE MACDONALD

(1824–1905) Scottish poet, novelist and lay preacher

George MacDonald served briefly as a Congregationalist minister in Arundel, Sussex, but was rejected by his congregation and so turned to literature while continuing as a lay preacher. He later became a member of the Church of England and was Editor of *Good Words for the Young.*

155

They all were looking for a king
　　To slay their foes, and lift them high:
Thou cam'st a little baby thing
　　That made a woman cry.

O son of man, to right my lot
　　Nought but thy presence can avail;
Yet on the road thy wheels are not,
　　Nor on the sea thy sail!

My fancied ways why should'st thou heed?
　　Thou com'st down thine own secret stair;
Com'st down to answer all my need,
　　Yea, every bygone prayer!

From *A Threefold Cord* (1883)

HARRIET MARTINEAU
(1802–76) English writer

Sister of the theologian James Martineau (q. v.), Harriet Martineau was a devout Unitarian in her youth. She wrote stories, novels and a variety of non-fiction as well as translating Comte's *Philosophie positive*. A friend of Wordsworth (q. v.) she was influenced by Bentham and J. S. Mill.

156

Lord Jesus! come; for here
Our path through wilds is laid;
We watch as for the day-spring near
Amid the breaking shade.

Lord Jesus! come; for hosts
Meet on the battle-plain:
The patriot mourns, the tyrant boasts,
And tears are shed like rain.

Lord Jesus! come; for still
Vice shouts her maniac mirth;
The famished crave in vain their fill,
While teems the fruitful earth.

Hark! herald-voices near
Lead on thy happier day:
Come, Lord, and our hosannas hear;
We wait to strew thy way.

Come, as in days of old,
With words of grace and power:
Gather us all within thy fold,
And never leave us more.

From *Hymns for the Christian Church and Home* (1840)
compiled by James Martineau (q. v.)

JAMES MARTINEAU

(1805–1900) English theologian and philosopher

Brother of Harriet Martineau (q. v.), James Martineau was a
Unitarian minister in Dublin and Liverpool before becoming
Professor of Mental and Moral Philosophy at Manchester New
College and was later its principal. One of the greatest
theologians of the nineteenth century, he also edited three
hymnbooks.

157

A voice upon the midnight air,
   Where Kedron's moonlit waters stray,
Weeps forth, in agony of prayer,
   'O Father, take this cup away!'

Ah, thou, who sorrowest unto death,
   We conquer in thy mortal fray;
And Earth for all her children saith,
   'O God, take not this cup away!'

O Lord of sorrow meekly die!
   Thou'lt heal or hallow all our woe;
Thy name refresh the mourner's sigh,
   Thy peace revive the faint and low.

Great Chief of faithful souls, arise!
   None else can lead the martyr-band,
Who teach the brave how peril flies
   When faith unarmed uplifts the hand.

O King of earth, the cross ascend!
   O'er climes and ages 'tis thy throne;
Where'er thy fading eye may bend
   The desert blooms, and is thine own.

Thy parting blessing, Lord, we pray:
Make but one fold below, above;
And when we go the last lone way,
O give the welcome of thy love!

From *Hymns for the Christian Church and Home* (1840)

HENRY HART MILMAN

(1791–1868) English poet and church historian

The son of Sir Francis Milman, Physician to George III, Henry Hart Milman won the Newdigate Prize for Poetry at Oxford University and after serving as Vicar of St Mary's, Reading, became Professor of Poetry at Oxford (1821–31), a Canon of Westminster Abbey (1835) and finally Dean of St Paul's Cathedral (1849).

158

Ride on! ride on in majesty!
Hark, all the tribes hosanna cry;
Thine humble beast pursues his road
With palms and scattered garments strowed.

Ride on! ride on in majesty!
In lowly pomp ride on to die:
O Christ, thy triumphs now begin
O'er captive death and conquered sin.

Ride on! ride on in majesty!
The wingèd squadrons of the sky
Look down with sad and wondering eyes
To see the approaching sacrifice.

Ride on! ride on in majesty!
Thy last and fiercest strife is nigh;
The Father, on his sapphire throne,
Expects his own anointed Son.

Ride on! ride on in majesty!
In lowly pomp ride on to die;
Bow thy meek head to mortal pain
Then take, O God, thy power, and reign.

First published in *Hymns* (1827) by Reginald Heber (q. v.)

159

O help us, Lord; each hour of need
   Thy heavenly succour give;
Help us in thought and word and deed,
   Each hour on earth we live.

O help us, when our spirits cry
   With contrite anguish sore;
And when our hearts are cold and dry,
   O help us, Lord, the more.

O help us through the prayer of faith
   More firmly to believe;
For still, the more the servant hath,
   The more shall he receive.

O help us, Saviour, from on high;
   We know no help but thee;
O help us so to live and die,
   As thine in heaven to be.

From *Selection of Psalms and Hymns* (1837)

JOHN MILTON
(1608–74) English poet

Born in London, Milton served as Secretary of Foreign
Tongues during the Cromwell administration but is best known
for his long religious poems, especially *Paradise Lost* (1667).

160

Let us with a gladsome mind
Praise the Lord, for he is kind,
   For his mercies ay endure,
   Ever faithful, ever sure.

Let us blaze his Name abroad,
For of gods he is the God;

O let us his praises tell,
That doth the wrathfull tyrants quell.

That with his miracles doth make
Amazed Heav'n and Earth to shake.

That by his wisdom did create
The painted Heav'ns so full of state.

That did the solid Earth ordain
To rise above the watry plain.

That by his all-commanding might,
Did fill the new-made world with light.

And caus'd the Golden-tressed Sun,
All the day long his cours to run.

The horned Moon to shine by night,
Amongst her spangled sisters bright.

He with his thunder-clasping hand,
Smote the first-born of *Egypt* Land.

And in despight of *Pharao* fell,
He brought from thence his *Israel.*

The ruddy waves he cleft in twain,
Of the Erythræan main.

The floods stood still like Walls of Glass,
While the Hebrew Bands did pass.

But fullsoon they did devour
The Tawny King with all his power.

His chosen people he did bless
In the wastfull Wildernes.

In bloody battail he brought down
Kings of prowess and renown.

He foild bold *Seon* and his host,
That rul'd the *Amorrean* coast.

And large lim'd *Og* he did subdue,
With all his hardy crew.

And to his Servant *Israel,*
He gave their Land therin to dwell.

He hath with a piteous eye
Beheld us in our misery.

And freed us from the slavery
Of the invading enimy.

All living creatures he doth feed,
And with full hand supplies their need.

Let us therefore warble forth
His mighty Majesty and worth.

That his mansion hath on high
Above the reach of mortall eye.

Based on Psalm 136, this hymn was written in 1623 when Milton was
aged fifteen and published in *Poems in Latin and English* (1645)

161

How lovely are thy dwellings fair!
   O Lord of Hosts, how dear
Thy pleasant tabernacles are,
   Where thou dost dwell so near.

My soul doth long and almost die
   Thy courts, O Lord, to see;
My heart and flesh aloud do cry,
   O living God, for thee.

There ev'n the sparrow freed from wrong
   Hath found a house of rest;
The swallow there, to lay her young
   Hath built her brooding nest.

Ev'n by thy altars, Lord of Hosts,
   They find their safe abode,
And home they fly from round the coasts
   Towards thee, my King, my God.

Happy who in thy house reside,
   Where thee they ever praise!
Happy whose strength in thee doth bide,
   And in their hearts thy ways.

They journey on from strength to strength
   With joy and gladsome cheer,
Till all before our God at length
   In Sion do appear.

For God, the Lord, both sun and shield,
   Gives grace and glory bright;
No good from them shall be withheld
   Whose ways are just and right.

Based on Psalm 84, from *Poems* (1673)

162

The Lord will come and not be slow,
    His footsteps cannot err;
Before him righteousness shall go,
    His royal harbinger.
Truth from the earth, like to a flower,
    Shall bud and blossom then;
And justice, from her heavenly bower,
    Look down on mortal men.

Surely to such as do him fear
    Salvation is at hand!
And glory shall ere long appear
    To dwell within our land.
Rise, God, judge thou the earth in might,
    This wicked earth redress;
For thou art he who shall by right
    The nations all possess.

The nations all whom thou hast made
    Shall come, and all shall frame
To bow them low before thee, Lord,
    And glorify thy Name.
For great thou art, and wonders great
    By thy strong hand are done:
Thou in thy everlasting seat
    Remainest God alone.

Based on Psalms 85, 82 and 86, published in *Poems* (1673)

JAMES MONTGOMERY

(1771–1854) Scottish poet and journalist

The son of a Moravian minister, Montgomery was intended for the church but later became Editor of the *Sheffield Iris* newspaper and was twice imprisoned in York Castle for his radical opinions. He wrote more than four hundred hymns.

163

Angels, from the realms of glory,
   Wing your flight o'er all the earth;
Ye who sang creation's story,
   Now proclaim Messiah's birth:
    Come and worship,
Worship Christ, the new-born King.

Shepherds, in the field abiding,
   Watching o'er your flocks by night,
God with man is now residing,
   Yonder shines the infant Light:
    Come and worship, etc.

Sages, leave your contemplations;
   Brighter visions beam afar:
Seek the great Desire of Nations;
   Ye have seen his natal star:
    Come and worship, etc.

Saints before the altar bending,
   Watching long in hope and fear,
Suddenly the Lord, descending,
   In his temple shall appear:
    Come and worship, etc.

Though an infant now we view him,
   He shall fill his Father's throne,
Gather all the nations to him;
   Every knee shall then bow down:
    Come and worship, etc.

From *Christian Psalmist* (1825)

164

Hail to the Lord's Anointed!
　Great David's greater Son;
Hail, in the time appointed,
　His reign on earth begun!
He comes to break oppression,
　To set the captive free,
To take away transgression,
　And rule in equity.

He comes in succour speedy
　To those who suffer wrong;
To help the poor and needy,
　And bid the weak be strong;
To give them songs for sighing,
　Their darkness turn to light,
Whose souls, condemned and dying,
　Were precious in his sight.

By such shall he be fearèd
　While sun and moon endure;
Beloved, obeyed, reverèd,
　For he shall judge the poor
Through changing generations,
　With justice, mercy, truth,
While stars maintain their stations,
　Or moons renew their youth.

He shall come down like showers
　Upon the fruitful earth,
And love, joy, hope, like flowers
　Spring in his path to birth:
Before him on the mountains,
　Shall Peace, the herald, go;
And righteousness, in fountains
　From hill to valley flow.

Arabia's desert ranger
　To him shall bow the knee.
The Ethiopian stranger
　His glory come to see.
With offerings of devotion,
　Ships from the isles shall meet,
To pour the wealth of ocean
　In tribute at his feet.

Kings shall bow down before him,
　And gold and silver bring:
All nations shall adore him,
　His praise all people sing:
For he shall have dominion
　O'er river, sea and shore,
Far as the eagle's pinion
　Or dove's light wing can soar.

For him shall prayer unceasing
　And daily vows ascend;
His kingdom still increasing,
　A kingdom without end:
The mountain dews shall nourish
　A seed in weakness sown,
Whose fruit shall spread and
　　flourish,
　And shake like Lebanon.

O'er every foe victorious,
　He on his throne shall rest,
From age to age more glorious
　All-blessing and all-blest:
The tide of time shall never
　His covenant remove;
His name shall stand for ever:
　That name to us is Love.

Based on Psalm 72, from *Songs of Zion* (1822)

✠ ✠ ✠

THOMAS MOORE
(1779–1852) Irish poet

A great friend of Lord Byron, Thomas Moore was born in Dublin and was appointed Registrar for the Admiralty Court in Bermuda (1803). A good musician, he also wrote songs as well as being the foremost Irish poet of his day.

165

Thou art, O God, the life and light
   Of all this wondrous world we see;
Its glow by day, its smile by night,
   Are but reflections caught from thee:
Where'er we turn, thy glories shine,
   And all things fair and bright are thine.

When day with farewell beam delays
   Among the opening clouds of even,
And we can almost think we gaze
   Through golden vistas into heaven,–
Those hues that make the sun's decline
   So soft, so radiant, Lord, are thine.

When night with wings of starry gloom
   O'ershadows all the earth and skies,
Like some dark beauteous bird whose plume
   Is sparkling with unnumbered eyes,–
That sacred gloom, those fires divine,
   So grand, so countless, Lord, are thine.

When youthful spring around us breathes,
   Thy Spirit warms her fragrant sigh,
And every flower the summer wreathes
   Is born beneath that kindling eye,–
Where'er we turn, thy glories shine,
   And all things fair and bright are thine.

From *Sacred Songs* (1816)

166

Thy heaven on which 'tis bliss to look,
Shall be my pure and shining book,
Where I shall read, in words of flame,
The glories of thy wondrous name.

There's nothing bright, above, below,
From flowers that bloom to stars that glow,
But in its light my soul can see
Some feature of thy deity:

There's nothing dark, below, above,
But in its gloom I trace thy love,
And meekly wait that moment when
Thy touch shall turn all bright again.

From *Sacred Songs* (1816)

HENRY MORE

(1614–87) English philosopher

A Fellow of Christ's College, Cambridge, Henry More was one
of a group known as the Cambridge Platonists (influenced by
the ancient Greek philosopher Plato and the Neoplatonists) who
tried to promote a rational form of Christianity. His works
greatly influenced John Wesley (q. v.) and Coleridge (q. v.).

167

The holy Son of God most high,
    For love of Adam's lapsèd race,
Quit the sweet pleasures of the sky
    To bring us to that happy place.

His robes of light he laid aside,
    Which did his majesty adorn,
And the frail state of mortals tried,
    In human flesh and figure born.

Whole choirs of angels loudly sing
  The mystery of his sacred birth,
And the blest news to shepherds bring,
  Filling their watchful souls with mirth.

The Son of God thus man became,
  That men the sons of God might be,
And by their second birth regain
  A likeness to his deity.

From *Divine Hymns* (1668)

✠ ✠ ✠

WILLIAM MORRIS

(1834–96) English craftsman and poet

William Morris had intended to take Holy Orders but later
turned to painting, handicrafts and writing, notably the long
narrative poem *The Earthly Paradise*. He was closely linked with
the pre-Raphaelite group of painters, including D. G. Rossetti,
brother of Christina Rossetti (q. v.).

168

Masters in this Hall,
  Hear ye new today
Brought from over sea,
  And ever I you pray:
Nowell! Nowell! Nowell!
Nowell sing we clear!
Holpen are all folk on earth,
Born is God's son so dear:
Nowell! Nowell!
Nowell sing we loud!
God today hath poor folk raised
And cast a-down the proud.

Going o'er the hills,
    Through the milk-white snow,
Heard I ewes bleat
    While the wind did blow:
Nowell! etc.

Shepherds many an one
    Sat among the sheep,
No man spake more word
    Than they had been asleep:
Nowell! etc.

Quoth I, 'Fellows mine,
    Why this guise sit ye?
Making but dull cheer,
    Shepherds though ye be?
Nowell! etc.

'Shepherds should of right
    Leap and dance and sing
Thus to see ye sit,
    Is a right strange thing':
Nowell! etc.

Quoth these fellows then,
    'To Bethlem town we go,
To see a mighty lord
    Lie in manger low':
Nowell! etc.

'How name ye this lord,
    Shepherds?' then said I,
'Very God,' they said,
    'Come from Heaven high':
Nowell! etc.

Then to Bethlem town
    We went two and two,
And in a sorry place
    Heard the oxen low:
Nowell! etc.

Therein did we see
    A sweet and goodly may
And a fair old man,
    Upon the straw she lay:
Nowell! etc.

And a little child
    On her arm had she,
'Wot ye who this is?'
    Said the hinds to me:
Nowell! etc.

Ox and ass him know,
    Kneeling on their knee,
Wondrous joy had I
    This little babe to see:
Nowell! etc.

This is Christ the Lord,
    Masters be ye glad!
Christmas is come in,
    And no folk should be sad.
Nowell! etc.

CARDINAL JOHN HENRY NEWMAN
(1801–90) English theologian

John Henry Newman was a Fellow of Oriel College, Oxford, and later vicar of the university's church, St Mary the Virgin, before joining Keble (q. v.) and others to found the Oxford Movement or Tractarians. He later joined the Catholic Church and was elected a cardinal in 1879.

169

Lead, kindly Light, amid the encircling gloom,
    Lead thou me on;
The night is dark, and I am far from home,
    Lead thou me on.
Keep thou my feet; I do not ask to see
The distant scene; one step enough for me.

I was not ever thus, nor prayed that thou
    Should'st lead me on;
I loved to choose and see my path; but now
    Lead thou me on.
I loved the garish day, and, spite of fears,
Pride ruled my will: remember not past years.

So long thy power hath blessed me, sure it still
    Will lead me on,
O'er moor and fen, o'er crag and torrent, till
    The night is gone;
And with the morn those angel faces smile,
Which I have loved long since, and lost awhile.

From *Lyra Apostolica* (1830), this was a favourite hymn of Queen
Victoria and was read to her on her deathbed

170

Praise to the Holiest in the height,
    And in the depth be praise;
In all his words most wonderful,
    Most sure in all his ways.

O loving wisdom of our God!
    When all was sin and shame,
A second Adam to the fight
    And to the rescue came.

O wisest love! that flesh and blood,
    Which did in Adam fail,
Should strive afresh against the foe,
    Should strive and should prevail;

And that a higher gift than grace
    Should flesh and blood refine,
God's presence and his very self,
    And essence all-divine.

O generous love! that he, who smote
    In Man for man the foe,
The double agony in Man
    For man should undergo;

And in the garden secretly,
    And on the Cross on high,
Should teach his brethren, and inspire
    To suffer and to die.

Praise to the Holiest in the height,
    And in the depth be praise;
In all his words most wonderful,
    Most sure in all his ways.

From 'The Dream of Gerontius' in *Verses on Various Occasions* (1868)

171

Firmly I believe and truly
    God is Three, and God is One;
And I next acknowledge duly
    Manhood taken by the Son.

And I trust and hope most fully
    In that Manhood crucified;
And each thought and deed unruly
    Do to death, as he has died.

Simply to his grace and wholly
    Light and life and strength belong,
And I love supremely, solely,
    Him the holy, him the strong.

And I hold in veneration,
    For the love of him alone,
Holy Church as his creation,
    And her teachings as his own.

Adoration aye be given,
    With and through the angelic host,
To the God of earth and heaven,
    Father, Son, and Holy Ghost.

From 'The Dream of Gerontius' in *Verses on Various Occasions* (1868)

JOHN NEWTON
(1725–1807) English clergyman and poet

After an adventurous youth at sea as a slave-trader, Newton was Tide-Surveyor in Liverpool before taking Holy Orders and becoming Curate of Olney, Buckinghamshire. Here he later met Cowper (q. v.) and together they wrote the famous *Olney Hymns*. He became Rector of St Mary Woolnoth, London, in 1779.

172

Amazing grace! how sweet the sound
    That saved a wretch like me!
I once was lost, but now am found,
    Was blind, but now I see.

'Twas grace that taught my heart to fear,
    And grace my fears relieved;
How precious did that grace appear
    The hour I first believed.

Through many dangers, toils, and snares
    I have already come;
'Tis grace hath brought me safe thus far,
    And grace will lead me home.

The Lord has promised good to me,
    His word my hope secures;
He will my shield and portion be
    As long as life endures.

From *Olney Hymns* (1779)

173

Glorious things of thee are spoken,
    Zion, city of our God!
He whose word cannot be broken
    Formed thee for his own abode:
On the Rock of Ages founded,
    What can shake thy sure repose?
With salvation's walls surrounded,
    Thou may'st smile at all thy foes.

See, the streams of living waters,
    Springing from eternal love,
Well supply thy sons and daughters,
    And all fear of want remove:
Who can faint while such a river
    Ever flows their thirst to assuage?
Grace, which like the Lord the Giver,
    Never fails from age to age.

Round each habitation hov'ring,
    See the cloud and fire appear
For a glory and a cov'ring,
    Showing that the Lord is near.
Thus deriving from their banner
    Light by night and shade by day;
Safe they feed upon the manna
    Which he gives them when they pray.

Bless'd inhabitants of Zion,
   Wash'd in the Redeemer's blood!
Jesus, whom their hopes rely on,
   Makes them kings and priests to God.
'Tis his love his people raises
   Over self to reign as King,
And, as priests, his solemn praises
   Each for a thank-offering brings.

From 'Zion, or the City of God' in *Olney Hymns* (1779). Haydn was
very fond of this hymn and wrote the original music for it which was
subsequently used for the German national anthem.

174

How sweet the name of Jesus sounds
   In a believer's ear!
It soothes his sorrows, heals his wounds,
   And drives away his fear.

It makes the wounded spirit whole,
   And calms the troubled breast;
'Tis manna to the hungry soul,
   And to the weary rest.

Dear name! the rock on which I build,
   My shield and hiding-place,
My never-failing treasury filled
   With boundless stores of grace.

By thee my prayers acceptance gain,
   Although with sin defiled;
Satan accuses me in vain,
   And I am owned a child.

Jesus! my Shepherd, Husband, Friend,
   My Prophet, Priest, and King,
My Lord, my Life, my Way, my End,
   Accept the praise I bring.

Weak is the effort of my heart,
    And cold my warmest thought;
But when I see thee as thou art,
    I'll praise thee as I ought.

Till then I would thy love proclaim
    With every fleeting breath;
And may the music of thy name
    Refresh my soul in death.

         From *Olney Hymns* (1779)

175

Come, my soul, thy suit prepare:
Jesus loves to answer prayer;
He himself has bid thee pray,
Therefore will not say thee nay.

Thou art coming to a King:
Large petitions with thee bring;
For his grace and power are such
None can ever ask too much.

With my burden I begin:
Lord, remove this load of sin;
Let thy Blood, for sinners spilt,
Set my conscience free from guilt.

Lord, I come to thee for rest;
Take possession of my breast;
There thy blood-bought right maintain,
And without a rival reign.

While I am a pilgrim here,
Let thy love my spirit cheer;
Be my guide, my guard, my friend,
Lead me to my journey's end.

         From *Olney Hymns* (1779)

✣ ✣ ✣

ARTHUR WILLIAM EDGAR O'SHAUGHNESSY

(1841–81) English poet

At first a junior assistant in the British Library, O'Shaughnessy later became an expert on herpetology in the natural history department of the British Museum. He was a friend of D. G. Rossetti, brother of Christina Rossetti (q. v.).

176

With wonderful deathless ditties
We build up the world's great cities,
And out of a fabulous story
We fashion an empire's glory:
One man with a dream, at pleasure,
   Shall go forth and conquer a crown;
And three with a new song's measure
   Can trample a kingdom down.

A breath of our inspiration
Is the life of each generation;
A wondrous thing of our dreaming
Unearthly, impossible seeming–
The soldier, the king, and the peasant,
   Are working together in one,
Till our dream shall become their present,
   And their work in the world be done.

And therefore to-day is thrilling
With a past day's late fulfilling;
And the multitudes are enlisted
In the faith that their fathers resisted,
And, scorning the dream of to-morrow,
   Are bringing to pass, as they may,
In the world, for its joy or its sorrow,
   The dream that was scorned yesterday.

From *Moon and Moonlight* (1874)

FRANCIS TURNER PALGRAVE
(1824–97) English poet and critic

The eldest son of the historian Sir Francis Palgrave, F. T. Palgrave was a Fellow of Exeter College, Oxford, and briefly the Secretary of Gladstone (q. v.). Later Professor of Poetry at Oxford and art critic on the *Saturday Review*, he is best known for his anthology, *The Golden Treasury of Songs and Lyrics* (1864).

177

O thou not made with hands,
  Not throned above the skies,
Nor walled with shining walls,
  Nor framed with stones of price,
More bright than gold or gem,
God's own Jerusalem!

Thou art where'er the proud
  In humbleness melts down;
Where self itself yields up;
  Where martyrs win their crown;
Where faithful souls possess
Themselves in perfect peace.

Where'er the gentle heart
  Finds courage from above;
Where'er the heart forsook
  Warms with the breath of love;
Where faith bids fear depart,
City of God, thou art.

Where in life's common ways
  With cheerful tread we go;
Where in his steps we tread;
  Who trod the way of woe;
Where he is in the heart,
City of God, thou art.

Not throned above the skies,
  Nor golden-walled afar,
But where Christ's two or three
  In his name gathered are,
Lo, in the midst of them,
God's own Jerusalem!

From *Hymns* (1867)

178

Thou say'st, 'Take up thy cross,
O man, and follow me':
The night is black, the feet are slack,
Yet we would follow thee.

But O, dear Lord, we cry,
That we thy face could see,
Thy blessèd face one moment's space;
Then might we follow thee!

Dim tracts of time divide
Those golden days from me;
Thy voice comes strange o'er years of change;
How can I follow thee?

Comes faint and far thy voice
From vales of Galilee;
Thy vision fades in ancient shades;
How should we follow thee?

Ah, sense-bound heart and blind
Is nought but what we see?
Can time undo what once was true?
Can we not follow thee?

Within our heart of hearts
In nearest nearness be:
Set up thy throne within thine own: –
Go, Lord: we follow thee.

From *Hymns* (1867)

179

Lord God of morning and of night,
We thank thee for thy gift of light:
As in the dawn the shadows fly,
We seem to find thee now more nigh.

O Lord of light, 'tis thou alone
Canst make our darkened hearts thine own:
Though this new day with joy we see,
Great Dawn of God, we cry for thee.

Praise God our Maker and our Friend;
Praise him through time, till time shall end;
Till psalm and song his name adore
Through heaven's great day of Evermore.

From Hymns (1867)

ST PATRICK

(c. 372–466) Patron saint of Ireland

The son of a deacon, St Patrick was probably born in Wales and, seized by pirates, was taken to Ireland aged sixteen and sold as a slave. He later escaped to France, became a monk and then, having taken Holy Orders, returned to Ireland as a bishop to convert the people to Christianity. This version of the hymn ascribed to Patrick was translated from the Latin by Cecil Frances Alexander (1823–95), wife of Archbishop Alexander, Primate of All Ireland, and herself the author of many popular hymns such as 'Once in royal David's city', 'There is a green hill far away', etc.

180

I bind unto myself today
   The strong name of the Trinity,
By invocation of the same
   The Three in One and One in Three.

I bind this day to me for ever
   By power of faith, Christ's incarnation;
His baptism in Jordan river,
   His death on Cross for my salvation;
His bursting from the spicèd tomb,
   His riding up the heavenly way,
His coming at the day of doom
   I bind unto myself today.

I bind unto myself the power
    Of the great love of Cherubim;
The sweet 'Well done' in judgment hour,
    The service of the Seraphim,
Confessors' faith, Apostles' word,
    The Patriarchs' prayers, the prophets' scrolls,
All good deeds done unto the Lord
    And purity of virgin souls.

I bind unto myself today
    The virtues of the star-lit heaven,
The glorious sun's life-giving ray,
    The whiteness of the moon at even,
The flashing of the lightning free,
    The whirling wind's tempestuous shocks,
The stable earth, the deep salt sea
    Around the old eternal rocks.

I bind unto myself today
    The power of God to hold and lead,
His eye to watch, his might to stay,
    His ear to hearken to my need.
The wisdom of my God to teach,
    His hand to guide, his shield to ward;
The word of God to give me speech,
    His heavenly host to be my guard.

Against the demon snares of sin,
    The vice that gives temptation force,
The natural lusts that war within,
    The hostile men that mar my course;
Or few or many, far or nigh,
    In every place and in all hours,
Against their fierce hostility
    I bind to me those holy powers.

Against all satan's spells and wiles,
    Against false words of heresy,
Against the knowledge that defiles,
    Against the heart's idolatry,

Against the wizard's evil craft,
   Against the death-wound and the burning,
The choking wave, the poisoned shaft,
   Protect me, Christ, till thy returning.

Christ be with me, Christ within me,
   Christ behind me, Christ before me,
Christ beside me, Christ to win me,
   Christ to comfort and restore me.
Christ beneath me, Christ above me,
   Christ in quiet, Christ in danger,
Christ in hearts of all that love me,
   Christ in mouth of friend and stranger.

I bind unto myself the name,
   The strong name of the Trinity,
By invocation of the same,
   The Three in One and One in Three.
Of whom all nature hath creation,
   Eternal Father, Spirit, Word:
Praise to the Lord of my salvation,
   Salvation is of Christ the Lord.

ALEXANDER POPE

(1688–1744) English poet

A Catholic by birth, Pope's many famous works included the 'Epistle of Eloisa to Abelard', a poem based on the tragic love-affair of the heretical theologian Peter Abelard (q. v.).

181

What conscience dictates to be done,
   Or warns me not to do,
This, teach me ever, Lord, to shun,
   That, ever to pursue.

If I am right, thy grace impart
   Still in the right to stay;
If I am wrong, O teach my heart
   To find that better way.

Save me alike from foolish pride,
   Or impious discontent
At aught thy wisdom has denied,
   Or aught thy goodness lent.

Teach me to feel another's woe,
   To hide the fault I see;
The mercy I to others show,
   That mercy show to me.

Based on the Lord's Prayer from *Essay on Man* (1738)

182

Vital spark of heav'nly flame!
Quit, oh quit this mortal frame:
Trembling, hoping, ling'ring, flying,
Oh the pain, the bliss of dying!
Cease, fond Nature, cease thy strife,
And let me languish into life.

Hark! they whisper; Angels say,
Sister spirit, come away.
What is this absorbs me quite?
Steals my senses, shuts my sight,
Drowns my spirits, draws my breath?
Tell me, my Soul, can this be Death?

The world recedes; it disappears!
Heav'n opens on my eyes! my ears
   With sounds seraphic ring:
Lend, lend your wings! I mount! I fly!
O Grave! where is thy Victory?
   O Death! where is thy Sting?

This ode, entitled 'The Dying Christian to His Soul', was inspired by
verses allegedly said by Emperor Hadrian on his deathbed

AURELIUS CLEMENS PRUDENTIUS
(348–*c.* 413) Spanish poet

One of the most important Latin Christian poets working during
the Roman Empire, Prudentius spent his career as a judge and as
an official in the Imperial Court before becoming a monk aged
fifty-seven, devoting himself to writing religious poetry.

183

Earth has many a noble city;
    Bethlehem, thou dost all excel.
Out of thee the Lord from heaven
    Came to rule his Israel.

Fairer than the sun at morning
    Was the star that told his birth,
To the world its God announcing
    Seen in fleshly form on earth.

Eastern sages at his cradle
    Make oblations rich and rare;
See them give, in deep devotion,
    Gold and frankincense, and myrrh.

Sacred gifts of mystic meaning:
    Incense doth their God disclose,
Gold the King of Kings proclaimeth
    Myrrh his sepulchre foreshows.

Jesu, whom the Gentiles worshipped
    At thy glad Epiphany,
Unto thee, with God the Father
    And the Spirit, glory be.

From *Liber Cathemerinon*
translated by Edward Caswall

184

Of the Father's love begotten
   Ere the worlds began to be,
He is Alpha and Omega,
   He the source, the ending he,
Of the things that are, that have been,
   And that future years shall see,
     Evermore and evermore.

At his word they were created;
   He commanded; it was done:
Heaven and earth and depths of ocean
   In their threefold order one;
All that grows beneath the shining
   Of the light of moon and sun,
     Evermore and evermore.

O that birth for ever blessèd!
   When the Virgin, full of grace,
By the Holy Ghost conceiving,
   Bare the Saviour of our race,
And the Babe, the world's Redeemer,
   First revealed his sacred face,
     Evermore and evermore.

O ye heights of heaven, adore him;
   Angel-hosts his praises sing;
Powers, dominions, bow before him,
   And extol our God and King:
Let no tongue on earth be silent,
   Every voice in concert ring,
     Evermore and evermore.

This is he whom seers and sages
   Sang of old with one accord;
Whom the writings of the Prophets
   Promised in their faithful word;
Now he shines, the long-expected:
   Let creation praise its Lord,
     Evermore and evermore.

Hail, thou Judge of souls departed!
   Hail, thou King of them that live!

On the Father's throne exalted
   None in might with thee may strive;
Who at last in judgement coming
   Sinners from thy face shalt drive,
      Evermore and evermore.

Now let old and young men's voices
   Join with boys' thy name to sing,
Matrons, virgins, little maidens
   In glad chorus answering;
Let their guileless songs re-echo,
   And the heart its praises bring,
      Evermore and evermore.

Christ, to thee, with God the Father,
   And, O Holy Ghost, to thee,
Hymn and chant and high thanksgiving
   And unwearied praises be,
Honour, glory, and dominion,
   And eternal victory,
      Evermore and evermore.

From *Liber Cathemerinon* translated by J. M. Neale

FRANCIS QUARLES
(1592–1644) English poet

After studying at Cambridge University and Lincoln's Inn, Quarles became Cup-bearer to James I's eldest daughter Princess Elizabeth, wife of Frederick V, Elector Palatinate. He was later Secretary to James Ussher, Archbishop of Armagh, and Chronologer to the City of London. His son John also wrote hymns and religious works.

185

Thou art my life; if thou but turn away
My life's a thousand deaths: thou art my way;
Without thee, Lord, I travel not, but stray.

My light thou art; without thy glorious sight
My eyes are darkened with perpetual night:
My God, thou art my way, my life, my light.

Thou art my way; I wander, if thou fly:
Thou art my light; if hid, how blind am I!
Thou art my life; if thou withdraw, I die.

Disclose thy sunbeams; close thy wings and stay;
See, see how I am blind, and dead, and stray,
O thou that art my light, my life, my way!

From *Emblemes* (1635)

CHRISTINA GEORGINA ROSSETTI
(1830–94) English poet

Daughter of a professor of Italian at King's College, London, and sister of the poet and painter D. G. Rossetti (she was the model for the Virgin Mary in *Ecce Ancilla Domini*), Christina Rossetti was a devout High Anglican much influenced by the Tractarians. As well as poetry she also wrote a number of devotional books.

186

In the bleak mid-winter
    Frosty wind made moan;
Earth stood hard as iron,
    Water like a stone;
Snow had fallen, snow on snow,
    Snow on snow,
In the bleak mid-winter,
    Long ago.

Our God, heaven cannot hold him
    Nor earth sustain;
Heaven and earth shall flee away
    When he comes to reign:
In the bleak mid-winter
    A stable-place sufficed
The Lord God almighty,
    Jesus Christ.

Enough for him, whom cherubim
   Worship night and day,
A breastful of milk
   And a mangerful of hay;
Enough for him, whom angels
   Fall down before,
The ox and ass and camel
   Which adore.

Angels and archangels
   May have gathered there,
Cherubim and seraphim
   Thronged the air;
But only his mother
   In her maiden bliss
Worshipped the Belovèd
   With a kiss.

What can I give him,
   Poor as I am?
If I were a shepherd
   I would bring a lamb;
If I were a wise man
   I would do my part;
Yet what I can I give him–
   Give my heart.

Gustav Holst composed a tune especially for this poem

187

What are these that glow from afar,
These that lean over the golden bar,
Strong as the lion, pure as the dove,
With open arms, and hearts of love?
They the blessèd ones gone before,
They the blessèd for evermore,
Out of great tribulation they went
Home to their home of heaven content.

What are these that fly as a cloud,
With flashing heads and faces bowed,
In their mouths a victorious psalm,
In their hands a robe and a palm?
Welcoming angels these that shine,
Your own angel, and yours, and mine;
Who have hedged us, both day and night,
On the left hand and on the right.

Light above light, and bliss beyond bliss,
Whom words cannot utter, lo, who is this?
As a king with many crowns he stands,
And our names are graven upon his hands;
As a priest, with God-uplifted eyes,
He offers for us his sacrifice;
As the Lamb of God, for sinners slain,
That we too may live, he lives again.

God the Father give us grace
To walk in the light of Jesus' face;
God the Son give us a part
In the hiding-place of Jesus' heart;
God the Spirit so hold us up
That we may drink of Jesus' cup;
God almighty, God three in One,
God almighty, God alone.

From *Prince's Progress* (1856)

188

Service and strength, God's angels and archangels;
　　His seraphs fires, and lamps his cherubim:
Glory to God from highest and from lowest,
　　Glory to God in everlasting hymn
　　　　From all his creatures.

Princes that serve, and Powers that work his pleasure,
　　Heights that soar toward him, depths that sink toward him;
Flames fire out-flaming, chill beside his essence;
　　Insight all-probing, save where scant and dim
　　　　Toward its Creator.

Sacred and free, exultant in God's pleasure,
　　His will their solace, thus they wait on him,
And shout their shout of ecstasy eternal,
　　And trim their splendours that they burn not dim
　　　　Toward their Creator.

Wherefore with angels, wherefore with archangels,
   With lofty cherubs, loftier seraphim,
We laud and magnify our God almighty,
   And veil our faces rendering love to him
     With all his creatures.

From *Called to be Saints* (1881)

SIR WALTER SCOTT

(1771–1832) Scottish poet and novelist

Britain's most popular poet before Byron, Scott refused the
post of Poet Laureate and recommended Southey instead. The
first of these two hymns adapted from his works is a translation
of the *Dies Irae.*

189

That day of wrath, that dreadful day,
When heaven and earth shall pass away,
What power shall be the sinner's stay?
How shall he meet that dreadful day?

When, shrivelling like a parchèd scroll,
The flaming heavens together roll;
When louder yet, and yet more dread,
Swells the high trump that wakes the dead:

O on that day, that wrathful day,
When man to judgement wakes from clay,
Be thou, O Christ, the sinner's stay,
Though heaven and earth shall pass away.

From *The Lay of the Last Minstrel* (1805)

190

When Israel, of the Lord beloved,
   Out of the land of bondage came,
Her fathers' God before her moved,
   An awful guide, in smoke and flame.

By day, along the astonished lands
   The cloudy pillar glided slow;
By night, Arabia's crimsoned sands
   Returned the fiery column's glow.

But present still, though now unseen,
   When brightly shines the prosperous day,
Be thoughts of thee a cloudy screen
   To temper the deceitful ray.

And O, when stoops on Judah's path,
   In shade and storm, the frequent night,
Be thou, long-suffering, slow to wrath,
   A burning and a shining light.

From *Ivanhoe* (1817), Chapter 40

✠ ✠ ✠

WILLIAM SHAKESPEARE

(1564–1616) English dramatist and poet

This hymn is taken from Sonnet CXLVI in Shakespeare's
Sonnets (1609).

191

Poor Soul, the centre of my sinful earth,
   Fooled by these rebel powers that thee array,
Why dost thou pine within, and suffer dearth,
   Painting thy outward walls so costly gay?

Why so large cost, having so short a lease,
    Dost thou upon thy fading mansion spend?
Shall worms, inheritors of this excess,
    Eat up thy charge? Is this thy body's end?

Then, Soul, live thou upon thy servant's loss,
    And let that pine to aggravate thy store;
Buy terms divine in selling hours of dross;
    Within be fed, without be rich no more:

So shalt thou feed on death, that feeds on men,
And death once dead, there's no more dying then.

✣ ✣ ✣

PERCY BYSSHE SHELLEY

(1792–1822) English poet

The son of Sir Timothy Shelley, MP for Horsham, Sussex, Percy Shelley was expelled from Oxford University for circulating a pamphlet entitled 'The Necessity of Atheism'. His second wife was Mary Godwin, daughter of former Dissenting Minister and later atheist philosopher, William Godwin.

192

The world's great age begins anew,
    The golden years return,
The earth doth like a snake renew
    Her winter weeds outworn:
Heaven smiles, and faiths and empires gleam,
Like wrecks of a dissolving dream.

A brighter Hellas rears its mountains
    From waves serener far;
A new Peneus rolls his fountains
    Against the morning star.
Where fairer Tempès bloom, there sleep
Young Cyclads on a sunnier deep.

Another Athens shall arise,
   And to remoter time
Bequeath, like sunset to the skies,
   The splendour of its prime;
And leave, if nought so bright may live,
All earth can take or heaven can give.

From *Hellas* (1822). Hellas is Greece, Peneus a river that
runs through the vale of Tempe near Mount Olympus and
the Cyclads are the Cyclades islands.

SIR PHILIP SIDNEY

(1554–86) English diplomat, soldier and poet

The son of Sir Henry Sidney, Lord Deputy Governor of
Ireland, and nephew of Elizabeth I's favourite, the Earl of
Leicester, Sir Philip Sidney was sent on diplomatic missions for
the Elector Palatine and Emperor Rudolf II. He was later MP
for Kent, Governor of Flushing and patron of the poet Spenser
(q. v.). None of Sidney's poems were published in his lifetime.

193

O Lord, in me there lieth nought
   But to thy search revealèd lies;
     For when I sit
     Thou markest it,
   No less thou notest when I rise;
The closest closet of my thought
   Hath open windows to thine eyes.

Thou walkest with me when I walk;
   When to my bed for rest I go,
     I find thee there,
     And everywhere;
   Not youngest thought in me doth grow,
No, not one word I cast to talk,
   But, yet unuttered, thou dost know.

Do thou thy best, O secret night,
In sable veil to cover me;
The sable pall
Shall vainly fall
With day unmasked my night shall be:
For night is day and darkness light,
O Father of all lights, to thee.

From *The Psalms of David*. This hymn, based on Psalm 139, is now
believed to be almost certainly by his sister Mary, Countess of
Pembroke (1561–1621) as Sir Philip only wrote the first forty-two
psalms in the collection.

CHRISTOPHER SMART

(1722–71) English poet

A brilliant classical scholar at Cambridge University, Smart
was institutionalised as insane from 1759 to 1763 for his
compulsion to pray in public. (Dr Johnson famously
commented 'I'd as lief pray with Kit Smart as anyone else.')
His best known poem, *A Song of David*, was published on his
release but the unfinished work he described as 'my
Magnificat'– the *Jubilate Agno* – was not published until 1939.

194

All the scenes of nature quicken,
By the genial spirit fanned;
And the painted beauties thicken,
Coloured by the Master's hand;

Earth her vigour repossessing,
As the blasts are held in ward,
Blessing heaped and pressed on blessing,
Yield the measure of the Lord.

Cowslips seize upon the fallow,
    And the cardamine in white,
Where the cornflowers join the mallow,
    Joy and health and thrift unite.

Hark! aloud the blackbird whistles,
    With surrounding fragrance blest,
And the goldfinch in the thistles
    Makes provision for her nest.

Prayer and praise be mine employment
    Without grudging or regret:
Lasting life and long enjoyment
    Are not here, and are not yet.

195

Hosanna! Music is divine,
When in the praise the psalmists join
    And each good heart is warm;
Yea, joy is sweetest so renewed,
And all the rites of gratitude
    Are rapture to perform.

For God is magnitude immense;
His prowess is omnipotence
    That knows no date or end,
His wisdom infinitely great;
And all duration, depth and height,
    His mysteries transcend.

He the blue heaven in beauty shrouds,
And balances the plumy clouds
    Which for the rain he wrings;
He causes the mild dew to drop
And grass upon the mountain top
    In tufted verdure springs.

He laid the verdant turf to graze,
That earth the due supplies might raise
   Of annual food and wealth;
And fragrant herbs and flowers profuse
The seasons on the field produce
   For pleasure and for health.

He shall the broken heart repair,
And for all sickness and despair
   A cure in Christ provide;
And heal the wounded and the bruised,
His oil into their sores infused,
   And soothing balm applied.

Based on Psalm 147

196

Awake, arise! lift up thy voice,
   Which as a trumpet swell!
Rejoice in Christ! again rejoice,
   And on his praises dwell!

Let us not doubt, as doubted some,
   When first the Lord appeared;
But full of faith and reverence come,
   What time his voice is heard.

And even as John, who ran so well,
   Confess upon our knees
The Prince that locks up death and hell,
   And has himself the keys.

And thus through gladness and surprise
   The saints their Saviour treat;
Nor will they trust their ears and eyes
   But by his hands and feet.

Those hands of liberal love indeed
   In infinite degree,
Those feet still frank to move and bleed
   For millions and for me.

O Dead, arise! O Friendless, stand
   By seraphim adored!
O Solitude, again command
   Thy host from heaven restored!

197

We sing of God, the mighty source
Of all things, the stupendous force
   On which all strength depends,
From whose right arm, beneath whose eyes,
All period, power, and enterprise
   Commences, reigns, and ends.

Glorious the sun in mid career,
Glorious the assembled fires appear,
   Glorious the comet's train,
Glorious the trumpet and alarm,
Glorious the almighty stretched-out arm,
   Glorious the enraptured main.

The world, the clustering spheres he made,
The glorious light, the soothing shade,
   Dale, champaigne, grove, and hill,
The multitudinous abyss,
Where secrecy remains in bliss,
   And wisdom hides her skill.

Strong is the lion, like a coal
His eyeball, like a bastion's mole
   His chest against the foes:
Strong the gier-eagle on his sail;
Strong against tide the enormous whale
   Emerges as he goes;

But stronger still – in earth and air,
And in the sea – the man of prayer;
   And far beneath the tide,
And in the seat to faith assigned,
Where ask is have, where seek is find,
   Where knock is open wide.

✣ ✣ ✣

CAROLINE ANNE SOUTHEY
(1786–1854) English poet

Caroline Anne Bowles was born in Hampshire and wrote short stories and verse. She was a friend of the poet Southey for many years and eventually became his second wife.

198

Launch thy bark, mariner!
   Christian, God speed thee!
Let loose the rudder-bands;
   Good angels lead thee.
Set thy sails warily,
   Tempests will come;
Steer thy course steadily;
   Christian, steer home.

Look to the weather bow,
   Breakers are round thee;
Let fall the plummet now
   Shallows may ground thee.
Reef in the foresail there,
   Hold the helm fast:
So, – let the vessel wear;
   There swept the blast.

'What of the night, watchman?
   What of the night?'
'Cloudy, all quiet,
   No land yet – all's right.'
Be wakeful, be vigilant;
   Danger may be
At an hour when all seemeth
   Securest to thee.

How? gains the leak so fast?
   Clear out the hold;
Hoist up thy merchandise,
   Heave out thy gold.
There – let the ingots go;
   Now the ship rights:
Hurrah! the harbour's near;
   Lo! the red lights.

Slacken not sail yet
   At inlet or island;
Straight for the beacon steer,
   Straight for the highland.
Crowd all thy canvas on,
   Cut through the foam;
Christian, cast anchor now,
   Heaven is thy home!

'Mariner's Hymn' from *Solitary Hours* (1826)

✤ ✤ ✤

ST ROBERT SOUTHWELL

(*c.* 1561–95) English clergyman, poet and martyr

Southwell was educated by Jesuits, became a Roman Catholic priest and was chaplain to the Countess of Arundel. Imprisoned in the Tower, he was tortured and executed for high treason by Elizabeth I. His best known works are *St Peter's Complaint* (1595) and *The Burning Babe.*

199

Behoulde a sely tender Babe
   In freezing winter nighte,
In homely manger trembling lies:
   Alas, a piteous sighte:
The innes are full, no man will yelde
   This little Pilgrime bedd:
But forced He is with sely beastes
   In cribbe to shroude His headd.

Despise not Him for lying there,
   First what He is enquire:
An orient perle is often found
   In depth of dirty mire.
Waye not His cribbe, His wodden dishe,
   Nor beastes that by Him feede:
Waye not His Mother's poor attire,
   Nor Josephe's simple weede.

This stable is a Prince's courte,
   The cribbe His chaire of state:
The beastes are parcell of His pompe,
   The wodden dishe His plate.
The parsons in that poor attire
   His royall liveries weare:
The Prince Himself is come from heaven,
   This pompe is prised there.

With joye approch, O Christen wighte,
    Do homage to thy Kinge:
And highly prise this humble pompe,
    Which He from heaven doth bringe:
With joye approch, O Christen wighte,
    Do homage to thy Kinge:
And highly prise this humble pompe
    Which He from heaven doth bringe.

'New Prince, New Pompe' ('sely' means simple)

200

Let folly praise what fancy loves,
I praise and love that Child,
Whose heart no thought, whose tongue no word
Whose hand no deed defiled,
    I praise Him most, I love Him best,
    All praise and love is His;
    While Him I love, in Him I live,
    And cannot live amiss.

Love's sweetest mark, laud's highest theme,
Man's most desired delight;
To love Him life, to leave Him death,
To live in Him delight.
    He mine by gift, I His by debt,
    Thus each to other due,
    First friend He was, best friend He is,
    All times will find Him true.

Though young yet wise, though small yet strong,
Though Man yet God He is;
As wise He knows, as strong He can,
As God He loves to bless.
    His knowledge rules, His strength defends,
    His love doth cherish all;
    His birth our joy, His life our light,
    His death our end of thrall.

Alas! He weeps, He sighs, He pants,
　　Yet do His angels sing;
Out of His tears, His sighs, and throbs
　　Doth bud a joyful spring.
　　　　Almighty Babe, Whose tender arms
　　　　Can force all foes to fly,
　　　　Correct my faults, protect my life,
　　　　Direct me when I die.

✤ ✤ ✤

EDMUND SPENSER

(*c.* 1552–99) English poet

A close friend of Sir Philip Sidney (q. v.) Spenser was at first
Secretary to John Young, Bishop of Rochester, and later
Secretary to Lord Grey de Wilton, Lord Deputy of Ireland.
His best known poem is *The Faerie Queene.*

201

Most glorious Lord of life, that on this day
　　Didst make thy triumph over death and sin,
And having harrowed hell, didst bring away
　　Captivity thence captive, us to win:

This joyous day, dear Lord, with joy begin,
　　And grant that we, for whom thou diddest die,
Being with thy dear blood clean washed from sin,
　　May live for ever in felicity:

And that thy love we, weighing worthily,
　　May likewise love thee for the same again;
And for thy sake, that all like dear didst buy,
　　With love may one another entertain.

So let us love, dear Love, like as we ought,
　　Love is the lesson which the Lord us taught.

Sonnet LXVIII from *Amoretti and Epithalamion* (1595)

HARRIET BEECHER STOWE

(1812–96) American novelist

Best known for her anti-slavery book, *Uncle Tom's Cabin*, Harriet Beecher Stowe was the daughter of Lyman Beecher, leader of the New School Presbyterians, and the sister of the author and Congregationalist preacher Henry Ward Beecher. She married the Rev. C. E. Stowe, a Professor of Theology.

202

Still, still with thee, when purple morning breaketh,
　　When the bird waketh, and the shadows flee;
Fairer than morning, lovelier than the daylight,
　　Dawns the sweet consciousness, I am with thee.

As in the dawning, o'er the waveless ocean,
　　The image of the morning star doth rest,
So in this stillness, thou beholdest only
　　Thine image in the waters of my breast.

When sinks the soul, subdued by toil, to slumber,
　　Its closing eye looks up to thee in prayer;
Sweet the repose beneath the wings o'ershading,
　　But sweeter still to wake and find thee there.

So shall it be at last, in that bright morning
　　When the soul waketh, and life's shadows flee;
O, in that hour, fairer than daylight dawning,
　　Shall rise the glorious thought, I am with thee.

In H. W. Beecher (ed) *Plymouth Collection* (1855).

203

When winds are raging o'er the upper ocean,
　　And billows wild contend with angry roar,
'Tis said, far down beneath the wild commotion
　　That peaceful stillness reigneth evermore.

Far, far beneath, the noise of tempest dieth,
   And silver waves chime ever peacefully;
And no rude storm, how fierce soe'er he flieth,
   Disturbs the sabbath of that deeper sea.

So to the soul that knows thy love, O Purest,
   There is a temple, peaceful evermore;
And all the babble of life's angry voices
   Dies in hushed stillness at its sacred door.

Far, far away, the noise of passion dieth,
   And loving thoughts rise ever peacefully;
And no rude storm, how fierce soe'er he flieth,
   Disturbs that deeper rest, O Lord, in thee.

In H. W. Beecher (ed.) *Plymouth Collection* (1855)

ALGERNON CHARLES SWINBURNE
(1837–1909) English poet

Algernon Charles Swinburne was the eldest son of Admiral
Swinburne and a friend of D. G. Rossetti (brother of Christina
Rossetti, q. v.) and William Morris (q. v.). A number of his
poems have been made into hymns.

204

Thou whose birth on earth
   Angels sang to men,
While thy stars made mirth,
Saviour, at thy birth,
   This day born again;

As this night was bright
   With thy cradle-ray,
Very light of light,
Turn the wild world's night
   To thy perfect day.

Thou, the Word and Lord,
   In all time and space
Heard, beheld, adored,
With all ages poured
   Forth before thy face,

Lord, what worth in earth
   Drew thee down to die?
What therein was worth,
Lord, thy death and birth?
   What beneath thy sky?

Yet thy poor endure,	Bid our peace increase,
And are with us yet.	Thou that madest morn;
Be thy name a sure	Bid oppressions cease;
Refuge for thy poor,	Bid the night be peace;
Whom men's eyes forget.	Bid the day be born!

From *Songs Before Sunrise* (1871)

✛ ✛ ✛

JOHN ADDINGTON SYMONDS
(1840–93) English poet and writer

Winner of the Newdigate Prize for Poetry while an under-
graduate at Oxford University, Symonds was later a Fellow of
Magdalen College. However, tuberculosis later forced him to
move to Switzerland.

205

To God, the everlasting, who abides,
　One Life within things infinite that die;
To him whose unity no thought divides:
　Whose breath is breathèd through immensity.

Him neither eye hath seen, nor ear hath heard;
　Nor reason, seated in the souls of men,
Though pondering oft on the mysterious word,
　Hath e'er revealed his Being to mortal ken.

Only we feel him; and in aching dreams,
　Swift intuitions, pangs of keen delight,
The sudden vision of his glory seems
　To sear our souls, dividing the dull night:

And we yearn toward him: Beauty, Goodness, Truth,
　These three are one; one life, one thought, one being;
One source of still rejuvenescent youth;
　One light for endless and unclouded seeing.

O God, unknown, invisible, secure,
   Whose Being by dim resemblances we guess,
Who in man's fear and love abidest sure,
   Whose power we feel in darkness and confess!

       From 'An Invocation' in *Many Moods* (1878)

206

These things shall be! A loftier race
   Than e'er the world hath known, shall rise
With flame of freedom in their souls
   And light of science in their eyes.

They shall be gentle, brave, and strong,
   To spill no drop of blood, but dare
All that may plant man's lordship firm
   On earth and fire and sea and air.

They shall be simple in their homes
   And splendid in their public ways,
Filling the mansions of the state
   With music and with hymns of praise.

Nation with nation, land with land,
   Inarmed shall live as comrades free;
In every heart and brain shall throb
   The pulse of one fraternity.

New arts shall bloom of loftier mould,
   And mightier music thrill the skies,
And every life shall be a song,
   When all the earth is paradise.

       From 'A Vista' in *New and Old* (1880)

SYNESIUS OF CYRENE

(*c*. 375–430) Greek philosopher, poet and clergyman

Born in Cyrene, Synesius studied in Alexandria under the brilliant female philosopher Hypatia (immortalised in the romance, *Hypatia*, by Charles Kingsley q. v.). He turned Christian *c*. 401 and later became Bishop of Ptolemais.

207

Lord Jesus, think on me
And purge away my sin;
From earthborn passions set me free,
And make me pure within.

Lord Jesus, think on me,
With care and woe opprest;
Let me thy loving servant be,
And taste thy promised rest.

Lord Jesus, think on me
Amid the battle's strife;
In all my pain and misery
Be thou my health and life.

Lord Jesus, think on me,
Nor let me go astray;
Through darkness and perplexity
Point thou the heavenly way.

Lord Jesus, think on me
When flows the tempest high:
When on doth rush the enemy,
O Saviour, be thou nigh.

Lord Jesus, think on me,
That, when the flood is past,
I may the eternal brightness see,
And share thy joy at last.

Translated by Allen William Chatfield in his *Songs and Hymns of the Earliest Greek Christian Poets* (1876)

NAHUM TATE

(1652–1715) Irish dramatist and poet

The son of an Irish clergyman, Tate became Poet Laureate in 1690 and Historiographer Royal in 1702. As well as plays and translations, he wrote Part 2 of *Absalom and Achitophel* with Dryden (q. v.) and the libretto to Purcell's *Dido and Aeneas*. In addition he produced, with Royal Chaplain Nicholas Brady, a metrical version of the Psalms known as the *New Version* (1696).

208

While shepherds watched their flocks by night,
    All seated on the ground,
The angel of the Lord came down,
    And glory shone around.

'Fear not,' said he, for mighty dread
    Had seized their troubled mind;
'Glad tidings of great joy I bring
    To you and all mankind.

'To you in David's town this day
    Is born of David's line
The Saviour, who is Christ the Lord;
    And this shall be the sign:

'The heavenly babe you there shall find
    To human view displayed,
All meanly wrapt in swathing bands,
    And in a manger laid.'

Thus spake the seraph; and forthwith
    Appeared a shining throng
Of angels praising God, and thus
    Addressed their joyful song:

'All glory be to God on high,
    And to the earth be peace;
Goodwill henceforth from heaven to men
    Begin and never cease.'

From the Supplement to the *New Version* (1700)

209

As pants the hart for cooling streams
    When heated in the chase;
So longs my soul, O God, for thee
    And thy refreshing grace.

For thee, my God, the living God,
    My thirsty soul doth pine;
O when shall I behold thy face,
    Thou Majesty divine?

Tears are my constant food, while thus
    Insulting foes upbraid,
'Deluded wretch, where's now thy God,
    And where thy promis'd aid?'

I sigh whene'er my musing thoughts
    Those happy days present,
When I with troops of pious friends
    Thy temple did frequent;

When I advanc'd with songs of praise
    My solemn vows to pay,
And led the joyful sacred throng
    That kept the festal day.

Why restless, why cast down, my soul?
   Trust God, and he'll employ
His aid for thee, and change these sighs
   To thankful hymns of joy.

My soul's cast down, O God, and thinks
   On thee and Sion still;
From Jordan's banks, from Hermon's heights,
   And Missar's humbler hill.

One trouble calls another on
   And bursting o'er my head,
Fall spouting down, till round my soul
   A roaring sea is spread.

But when thy presence, Lord of life,
   Has once dispelled this storm,
To thee I'll midnight anthems sing,
   And all my vows perform.

God of my strength, how long shall I,
   Like one forgotten, mourn?
Forlorn, forsaken and expos'd
   To my oppressors' scorn.

My heart is pierced as with a sword,
   Whilst thus my foes upbraid,
'Vain boaster, where is now thy God?
   And where his promised aid?'

Why restless, why cast down, my soul?
   Hope still; and thou shalt sing
The praise of him who is thy God,
   Thy health's eternal spring.

      Based on Psalm 42 in the *New Version* (1696)

210

Through all the changing scenes of life,
   In trouble and in joy,
The praises of my God shall still
   My heart and tongue employ.

Of his deliverance I will boast
    Till all that are distress'd
From my example courage take
    And soothe their griefs to rest.

O magnify the Lord with me,
    With me exalt his name:
When in distress to him I called,
    He to my rescue came.

Their drooping hearts were soon refreshed,
    Who looked to him for aid;
Desired success in every face,
    A cheerful air displayed.

'Behold,' say they. 'Behold the man
    Whom providence relieved,
The man so dangerously beset,
    So wondrously retrieved!'

The hosts of God encamp around
    The dwellings of the just:
Deliverance he affords to all
    Who on his succour trust.

O make but trial of his love;
    Experience will decide
How blest they are, and only they,
    Who in his truth confide.

Fear him, ye saints. and you will then
    Have nothing else to fear;
Make you his service your delight,
    Your wants shall be his care.

While hungry lions lack their prey,
    The Lord will food provide
For such as put their trust in him,
    And see their needs supplied.

Based on Psalm 34 in the *New Version* (1696)

ALFRED, LORD TENNYSON
(1809–92) English poet

Alfred Tennyson was the third surviving son of the Rector of
Somersby, Lincolnshire. He won the Chancellor's Medal for
English Verse at Trinity College, Cambridge, and his first
poems were published in *Poems by Two Brothers*, which also
featured verse by his brothers Frederick (q. v.) and Charles. He
succeeded Wordsworth (q. v.) as Poet Laureate in 1850.

211

Strong Son of God, immortal love,
　　Whom we, that have not seen thy face,
　　By faith, and faith alone, embrace,
Believing where we cannot prove;

Thou wilt not leave us in the dust:
　　Thou madest man, he knows not why;
　　He thinks he was not made to die;
And thou has made him; thou art just.

Thou seemest human and divine,
　　The highest, holiest manhood, thou;
　　Our wills are ours, we know not how;
Our wills are ours, to make them thine.

Our little systems have their day;
　　They have their day and cease to be;
　　They are but broken lights of thee,
And thou, O Lord, art more than they.

We have but faith: we cannot know;
　　For knowledge is of things we see;
　　And yet we trust it comes from thee,
A beam in darkness; let it grow.

Let knowledge grow from more to more,
　　But more of reverence in us dwell;
　　That mind and soul, according well,
May make one music as before,

But vaster. We are fools and slight;
    We mock thee when we do not fear;
    But help thy foolish ones to bear–
Help thy vain worlds to bear thy light.

From *In Memoriam* (1850)

212

    Sunset and evening star
  And one clear call for me!
And may there be no moaning of the bar,
    When I put out to sea.
But such a tide as, moving, seems asleep,
    Too full for sound and foam,
When that which drew from out the boundless deep
      Turns again home.

    Twilight and evening bell,
    And after that the dark!
And may there be no sadness of farewell,
    When I embark;
For though from out our bourne of time and place
    The flood may bear me far,
I hope to see my Pilot face to face
      When I have crossed the bar.

'Crossing the Bar' (this poem was always published at the end of
Tennyson's collected verse by his own request)

213

    Ring out, wild bells, to the wild sky,
    The flying cloud, the frosty light:
    The year is dying in the night;
Ring out, wild bells, and let him die.

    Ring out the grief that saps the mind,
    For those that here we see no more;
    Ring out the feud of rich and poor,
Ring in redress to all mankind.

Ring out a slowly dying cause,
   And ancient forms of party strife;
   Ring in the nobler modes of life,
With sweeter manners, purer laws.

Ring out false pride in place and blood,
   The civic slander and the spite;
   Ring in the love of truth and right,
Ring in the common love of good.

Ring out old shapes of foul disease;
   Ring out the narrowing lust of gold;
   Ring out the thousand wars of old,
Ring in the thousand years of peace.

Ring in the valiant man and free,
   The larger heart, the kindlier hand;
   Ring out the darkness of the land,
Ring in the Christ that is to be.

From *In Memoriam* (1850)

FREDERICK TENNYSON
(1807–98) English poet

Eldest surviving son of the Rector of Somersby, Lincolnshire, and brother of Alfred Lord Tennyson (q. v.), Frederick Tennyson won the Browne Medal for Greek Verse at Trinity College, Cambridge, and his first poems were published in *Poems by Two Brothers*, which also featured verse by his brothers Alfred and Charles.

214

The night is ended and the morning nears;
    Awake, look up, I hear the gathering sound
    Of coming cycles, like an ocean round;
I see the glory of a thousand years
    Lightening from bound to bound.

The hour is come again; the world-wide voice
    Of God shall cry into the ears of time;
    Scorners shall seek, and saints shall welcome him,
And know the ancient presence, and rejoice
    As in the days of prime.

And they that dwell apart shall know each other,
    And they that hymn their solemn songs alone
    Shall hear far voices mingling with their own,
And understand the utterance of a brother
    In every tongue and tone.

That note shall soar from every living heart;
    That endless note shall never die away.
    God, only God, to-day as yesterday,
Thou wert from everlasting, and thou art
    For ever and for ay.

From *Poems of the Day and Year* (1895)

ST THEODULPH OF ORLEANS

(d. 821) Italian monk

Born in Italy, Theodulph became an abbot of a monastery in Florence before being brought to France by Charlemagne (q. v.) where he became Bishop of Orléans. He was later imprisoned in a monastery in Angers by Emperor Louis the Pious who suspected him of conspiracy. His famous hymn was supposedly composed while in prison.

215

All glory, laud, and honour
  To thee, Redeemer, King,
To whom the lips of children
  Made sweet Hosannas ring.

Thou art the King of Israel,
  Thou David's royal Son,
Who in the Lord's name comest,
  The King and blessèd one.
    All glory, etc.

The company of angels
  Are praising thee on high,
And mortal men and all things
  Created make reply.
    All glory, etc.

The people of the Hebrews
  With palms before thee went:
Our praise and prayer and anthems
  Before thee we present.
    All glory, etc.

To thee before thy Passion
  They sang their hymns of praise:
To thee now high exalted
  Our melody we raise.
    All glory, etc.

Thou didst accept their praises,
  Accept the prayers we bring,
Who in all good delightest,
  Thou good and gracious King.
    All glory, etc.

Thy sorrow and thy triumph
  Grant us, O Christ, to share,
That to the holy city
  Together we may fare.
    All glory, etc.

For homage may we bring thee
  Our victory o'er the foe,
That in the Conqueror's triumph
  This strain may ever flow:
    All glory, etc.

Translated by J. M. Neale in *Hymnal Noted* (1854)

✜ ✜ ✜

ST THOMAS À KEMPIS
(1380–1471) German monk and scholar

Thomas Hammerken was born in Kempen (Kempis), Germany, entered an Augustinian monastery near Zwolle in 1400 and took Holy Orders in 1413. He later became successively Sub-prior and Superior of Mount St Agnes monastery and is best known as the author of *The Imitation of Christ*.

216

Jerusalem luminosa

Light's abode, celestial Salem,
    Vision whence true peace doth spring,
Brighter than the heart can fancy,
    Mansion of the highest King;
O how glorious are the praises
    Which of thee the prophets sing!

There for ever and for ever
    Alleluia is outpoured;
For unending, for unbroken,
    Is the feast-day of the Lord;
All is pure and all is holy
    That within thy walls is stored.

There no cloud nor passing vapour
    Dims the brightness of the air;
Endless noon-day, glorious noon-day,
    From the Sun of suns is there;
There no night brings rest from labour,
    For unknown are toil and care.

O how glorious and resplendent,
    Fragile body, shalt thou be,
When endued with so much beauty,
    Full of health, and strong, and free,
Full of vigour, full of pleasure
    That shall last eternally!

Now with gladness, now with courage,
  Bear the burden on thee laid,
That hereafter these thy labours
  May with endless gifts be paid,
And in everlasting glory
  Thou with joy may'st be arrayed.

Laud and honour to the Father,
  Laud and honour to the Son,
Laud and honour to the Spirit,
  Ever Three and ever One,
Consubstantial, co-eternal,
  While unending ages run.

Translated by J. M. Neale in *Hymnal Noted* (1854)

217
In domo Patris

Our Father's home eternal,
  O Christ, thou dost prepare
With many divers mansions,
  And each one passing fair:
They are the victors' guerdon
  Who, through the hard-won fight,
Have followed in thy footsteps
  And reign with thee in light.

Amid the happy number
  The virgins' crown and queen,
The ever-Virgin Mother,
  Is first and foremost seen:
Her one and only gladness,
  That undefilèd one,
To gaze in adoration,
  The Mother on the Son.

There Adam leads the chorus,
  And tunes the joyous strain
Of all his myriad children
  That follow in thy train:
Victorious over sorrow,
  The countless band to see,
Destroyed through his transgression,
  But raised to life through thee.

The patriarchs in their triumph
  Thy praises nobly sing,
Of old their promised offspring.
  And now their Victor-King;
The prophets harp their gladness
  That, whom their strains foretold,
In manifested glory
  They evermore behold.

And David calls to memory
  His own especial grace
In such clear prophet-vision
  To see thee face to face:
The apostolic cohort,
  Thy valiant and thine own,
As royal co-assessors
  Are nearest to thy throne.

Thy martyrs reign in glory
  Who triumphed as they fell,
And by a thousand tortures
  Defeated death and hell;
And every patient sufferer,
  Who sorrow dared contemn,
For each especial anguish
  Hath one especial gem.

The valiant-souled confessors
  Put on their meet array,
Who bare the heat and burden
  Of many a weary day:
The scorners of life's pleasures,
  Their self-denial ceased,
Sit down with thee and banquet
  At thy eternal feast.

The virgins walk in beauty
  Amidst their lily-bowers,
The coronals assuming
  Of never-fading flowers;
And innocents sport gaily
  Through all the courts of light,
To whom thou gav'st the guerdon
  Before they fought the fight.

The soldiers of thine army,
  Their earthly struggles o'er,
With joy put off the armour
  That they shall need no more:
For these and all that battled
  Beneath their Monarch's eyes,
The harder was the conflict
  The brighter is the prize.

The penitent, attaining
  Full pardon in thy sight,
Leave off the vest of sackcloth
  And don the robe of white:
The bondsman and the noble,
  The peasant and the king,
All gird one glorious Monarch
  In one eternal ring.

Translated by J. M. Neale in *Medieval Hymns* (1865)

FRANCIS THOMPSON
(1859–1907) English poet

The son of a doctor, Francis Thompson was brought up a Roman Catholic and was intended at first for the priesthood. Unsuited for this, he studied medicine but failed to graduate. A TB sufferer and opium addict, he took up literature while recovering from ill health in a monastery in Sussex where he wrote his most famous poem, *The Hound of Heaven*.

218

O world invisible, we view thee,
O world intangible, we touch thee,
O world unknowable, we know thee,
Inapprehensible, we clutch thee!

Does the fish soar to find the ocean,
The eagle plunge to find the air–
That we ask of the stars in motion
If they have rumour of thee there?

Not where the wheeling systems darken,
And our benumbed conceiving soars!–
The drift of pinions, would we hearken,
Beats at our own clay-shuttered doors.

The angels keep their ancient places;–
Turn but a stone and start a wing!
'Tis ye, 'tis your estrangèd faces,
That miss the many-splendoured thing.

Yea, in the night, my Soul, my daughter,
Cry – clinging Heaven by the hems;
And lo, Christ walking on the water
Not of Gennesareth, but Thames!

From *The Selected Poems of Francis Thompson* (1908)

AUGUSTUS MONTAGUE TOPLADY
(1740–78) English clergyman

Ordained in 1762, Toplady was Vicar of Broad Hembury, Devon, before becoming Preacher in the chapel of French Calvinists in Leicester Fields, London. A fervent defender of Calvinism, he was involved in a long feud with John Wesley (q. v.). He is best known for the hymn below – one of the most popular of all time – described by Oliver Wendell Holmes (q. v.) as 'The Protestant *Dies Irae*'.

219

Rock of ages, cleft for me
Let me hide myself in thee;
Let the water and the blood,
From thy riven side which flowed,
Be of sin the double cure:
Cleanse me from its guilt and power.

Not the labours of my hands
Can fulfil thy law's demands;
Could my zeal no respite know,
Could my tears for ever flow,
All for sin could not atone:
Thou must save, and thou alone.

Nothing in my hand I bring;
Simply to thy cross I cling;
Naked, come to thee for dress;
Helpless, look to thee for grace;
Foul, I to the fountain fly;
Wash me, Saviour, or I die.

While I draw this fleeting breath,
When mine eyes are closed in death,
When I soar through tracts unknown,
See thee on thy judgment throne;
Rock of ages, cleft for me,
Let me hide myself in thee.

From *Psalms and Hymns* (1776). A great favourite with
Gladstone (q. v.) this hymn was also much loved by Prince Albert
who repeated it on his deathbed.

✣ ✣ ✣

THOMAS TRAHERNE
(1637–74) English poet and writer

The son of a shoemaker, Thomas Traherne was brought up by
Philip Traherne, Mayor of Hereford. Graduating from
Brasenose College, Oxford, he was Rector of Credenhill, near
Hereford, before becoming chaplain to Sir Orlando
Bridgeman, Lord Keeper of the Great Seal under Charles II.
A 'Christian Epicurean', his most important writings, *Poems*
and *Centuries of Meditations* were not discovered until the
twentieth century.

220

Sweet Infancy!
O heavenly fire! O sacred light!
How fair and bright!
How great am I
Whom the whole world doth magnify!

O heavenly joy!
O great and sacred blessedness
Which I possess!
So great a joy
Who did into my arms convey?

From God above
Being sent, the gift doth me enflame
   To praise his name;
   The stars do move,
The sun doth shine, to show his love.

   O how divine
Am I! To all this sacred wealth,
   This life and health,
   Who raised? Who mine
Did make the same? What hand divine!

✣ ✣ ✣

THOMAS TUSSER

(1524–80) English agricultural writer and poet

Once a chorister at St Paul's Cathedral, Tusser was educated at
Eton and Cambridge and was a musician employed by Lord
Paget before retiring to write the book on agriculture in verse
for which he is best known, *A Hundreth Good Pointes of Husbandrie*
(1587). He also introduced the culture of barley to England. His
works are the origins of many proverbs such as 'A pig in a poke',
'Dog in the manger' and 'A rolling stone gathers no moss'.

221

Let such (so fantastical) liking not this
Nor anything honest that ancient is,
Give place to the time, that so meet we do see
Appointed of God, as it seemeth to be.

At Christmas, good husbands have corn in the ground,
In barn, and in cellar, worth many a pound,
Things plenty in house (beside cattle and sheep);
All sent them (no doubt on) good houses to keep.

At Christmas, the hardness of winter doth rage,
A griper of all things, especially age;
Then likely poor people, the young with the old
Be sorest oppressèd with hunger and cold.

At Christmas, by labour is little to get;
That wanting, the poorest in danger are set:
What season, then, better of all the whole year,
Thy needy poor neighbour to comfort and cheer?

HENRY VAUGHAN

(1622–95) Welsh poet

The twin brother of the writer, alchemist and Rosicrucian, Thomas Vaughan, Henry called himself 'The Silurst' after the ancient British tribe which once inhabited his birthplace, Breconshire. With Donne (q. v.) one of the Metaphysical Poets, he worked as a doctor and his poems were largely overlooked until the nineteenth century.

222

King of mercy, King of love,
Thou my life, in whom I move,
Perfect what thou hast begun,
Let no night put out this sun.

That hereafter, when I look
O'er the sullied, sinful book,
I may find thy hand therein
Wiping out my shame and sin.

Grant I may, my chief desire
Long for thee, to thee aspire;
Let my youth, my bloom of days,
Be my comfort, and thy praise.

O it is thy only art
To reduce a stubborn heart,
And since thine is victory
Strong holds should belong to thee.

Lord, then take it, leave it not
Unto my dispose or lot;
Since I could not have it mine,
O my God, let it be thine.

From *Silex Scintillans* (1650)

223

My soul, there is a country
    Far beyond the stars
Where stands a wingèd sentry
    All skilful in the wars:

There above noise, and danger,
    Sweet peace sits crowned with smiles,
And one born in a manger
    Commands the beauteous files.

He is thy gracious friend,
    And – O my soul, awake!–
Did in pure love descend,
    To die here for thy sake.

If thou canst get but thither,
    There grows the flower of peace,
The Rose that cannot wither,
    Thy fortress and thy ease.

Leave then thy foolish ranges,
    For none can thee secure
But one, who never changes,
    Thy God, thy life, thy cure.

From *Silex Scintillans*, Book 2 (1655)

224

They are all gone into the world of light,
    And I alone sit lingering here;
Their very memory is fair and bright,
    And my sad thoughts doth clear.

I see them walking in an air of glory,
    Whose light doth trample on my days;
My days, which are at best but dull and hoary,
    Mere glimmering and decays.

Dear beauteous death! the jewel of the just,
  Shining nowhere but in the dark;
What mysteries do lie beyond thy dust,
  Could man outlook that mark!

And yet as angels in some brighter dreams
  Call to the soul when man doth sleep;
So some strange thoughts transcend our wonted themes,
  And into glory peep.

O Father of eternal life, and all
  Created glories under thee,
Resume thy spirit from this world of thrall
  Into true liberty.

From Silex Scintillans, Book 2 (1655)

225

Ah, my dear Lord! what couldst thou spy
In this impure, rebellious clay,
That made thee thus resolve to die
For those that kill thee every day?

O what strange wonders could thee move
To slight thy precious blood, and breath!
Sure it was Love, my Lord; for Love
Is only stronger far than death.

From 'The Incarnation and Passion'
in Silex Scintillans (1650)

ISAAC WATTS

(1674–1748) English clergyman, poet and logician

At first a tutor to the family of Sir John Hartopp, Watts became a much respected Nonconformist (Independent) pastor, preacher and author of *Logic*. When his health failed he lived with Sir Thomas Abney and devoted himself to writing. One of the greatest hymnwriters, some of his verses were parodied by Lewis Carroll in his 'Alice' books.

226

When I survey the wondrous Cross,
  Where the young Prince of Glory died,
My richest gain I count but loss,
  And pour contempt on all my pride.

Forbid it, Lord, that I should boast
  Save in the death of Christ my God;
All the vain things that charm me most,
  I sacrifice them to his blood.

See from his head, his hands, his feet,
  Sorrow and love flow mingled down;
Did e'er such love and sorrow meet,
  Or thorns compose so rich a crown?

His dying crimson, like a robe,
  Spreads o'er his body on the Tree;
Then am I dead to all the globe,
  And all the globe is dead to me.

Were the whole realm of nature mine,
  That were a present far too small;
Love so amazing, so divine,
  Demands my soul, my life, my all.

From *Hymns and Spiritual Songs* (1707), Matthew Arnold (q. v.)
and Arnold Bennett both thought this the finest hymn in
the English language

227

O God, our help in ages past,
    Our hope for years to come,
Our shelter from the stormy blast,
    And our eternal home.

Under the shadow of thy throne
    Thy saints have dwelt secure;
Sufficient is thine arm alone,
    And our defence is sure.

Before the hills in order stood,
    Or earth received her frame,
From everlasting thou art God,
    To endless years the same.

Thy Word commands our flesh to dust,
    Return, ye sons of men;
All nations rose from Earth at first,
    And turn to earth again.

A thousand ages in thy sight
    Are like an evening gone;
Short as the watch that ends the night
    Before the rising sun.

The busy tribes of flesh and blood,
    With all their lives and cares,
Are carried downwards by the flood
    And lost in following years.

Time, like an ever-rolling stream
    Bears all its sons away;
They fly, forgotten as a dream
    Dies at the opening day.

Like flow'ry fields the nations stand
    Pleas'd with the morning light;
The flowers beneath the Mower's hand
    Lie withering e'er 'tis night.

O God, our help in ages past,
    Our hope for years to come,
Be thou our guard while troubles last,
    And our eternal home.

Based on Psalm 90, this is from Psalms of David *(1719) and
appears in* Shirley *by Charlotte Brontë*

228

There is a land of pure delight,
    Where saints immortal reign,
Infinite day excludes the night,
    And pleasures banish pain.

There everlasting spring abides,
    And never-withering flowers,
Death, like a narrow sea, divides
    This heavenly land from ours.

Sweet fields beyond the swelling flood
    Stand dressed in living green;
So to the Jews old Canaan stood,
    While Jordan rolled between.

But timorous mortals start and shrink
    To cross the narrow sea,
And linger shivering on the brink,
    And fear to launch away.

O could we make our doubts remove,
    Those gloomy doubts that rise,
And see the Canaan that we love
    With unbeclouded eyes:

Could we but climb where Moses stood,
    And view the landscape o'er,
Not Jordan's stream, nor death's cold flood,
    Should fright us from the shore.

From Hymns and Spiritual Songs *(1707)*

229

Jesus shall reign where'er the sun
Does his successive journeys run;
His kingdom stretch from shore to shore,
Till moons shall wax and wane no more.

Behold the Islands with their Kings,
And Europe her best tribute brings,
From North to South the Princes meet
To pay their homage at his feet.

There Persia glorious to behold,
There India stands in Eastern Gold,
And barbarous nations at his word
Submit and bow and own their Lord.

For him shall endless pray'r be made,
And praises throng to crown his head;
His name like sweet perfume shall rise
With every morning sacrifice.

People and realms of every tongue
Dwell on his love with sweetest song;
And infant-voices shall proclaim
Their early blessings on his name.

Blessings abound where'er he reigns,
The prisoner leaps to lose his chains,
The weary find eternal rest,
And all the sons of want are blest.

Where he displays his healing power
Death and the curse are known no more;
In him the tribes of Adam boast
More blessings than their father lost.

Let every creature rise and bring
Peculiar honours to our king;
Angels descend with songs again,
And earth repeat the long *Amen*.

Based on Psalm 72 from *Psalms of David* (1719)

✛ ✛ ✛

CHARLES WESLEY

(1707–88) English clergyman and poet

The son of the Rector of Epworth, Lincolnshire, and younger brother of John Wesley (q. v.), founder of Methodism, Charles Wesley was Secretary to General Oglethorpe in Georgia, USA, before becoming an itinerant preacher until 1756. He wrote more than 6,500 hymns.

230

O for a thousand tongues to sing
   My dear Redeemer's praise!
The glories of my God and King,
   The triumphs of his grace.

My gracious Master, and my God,
   Assist me to proclaim,
To spread through all the earth abroad
   The honours of thy name.

Jesus, the name that charms our fears,
   That bids our sorrows cease;
'Tis music in the sinner's ears,
   'Tis life and health and peace!

He breaks the power of cancell'd sin;
   He sets the prisoner free;
His blood can make the foulest clean;
   His blood availed for me.

He speaks, and listening to his voice
   New life the dead receive,
The mournful, broken hearts rejoice,
   The humble poor *believe.*

Hear him, ye deaf, his praise, ye dumb,
   Your loosen'd tongues employ,
Ye blind, behold your Saviour come,
   And leap, ye lame, for joy.

Look unto him, ye nations, own
    Your God, ye fallen race!
Look; and be saved through faith alone,
    Be justified by grace!

See all your sins on Jesus laid;
    The Lamb of God was slain,
His soul was once an offering made
    For every *soul* of man.

Awake from guilty nature's sleep,
    And Christ shall give you light,
Cast all your sins into the deep,
    And wash the *Ethiop* white.

With me, your Chief, you then shall know,
    Shall feel your sins forgiven;
Anticipate your heaven below
    And own that love is heaven.

From John and Charles Wesley, *Hymns and Sacred Songs* (1740). This has
appeared as the first hymn in every edition of the *Methodist Hymn Book.*

231

Jesu, lover of my soul,
    Let me to thy bosom fly,
While the nearer waters roll,
    While the tempest still is high;
Hide me, O my Saviour, hide,
    Till the storm of life is past;
Safe into the haven guide,
    O receive my soul at last.

Other refuge have I none,
    Hangs my helpless soul on thee;
Leave, ah! leave me not alone,
    Still support and comfort me:
All my trust on thee is stayed,
    All my help from thee I bring;
Cover my defenceless head
    With the shadow of thy wing.

Wilt thou not regard my call?
    Wilt thou not accept my prayer?
Lo! I sink, I faint, I fall!
    Lo, on thee I cast my care!
Reach me out thy gracious hand!
    While I of thy strength receive,
Hoping against hope I stand,
    Dying, and behold I live.

Thou, O Christ, art all I want;
    More than all in thee I find;
Raise the fallen, cheer the faint,
    Heal the sick, and lead the blind.
Just and holy is thy name;
    I am all unrighteousness.
False and full of sin I am;
    Thou art full of truth and grace.

Plenteous grace with thee is found.
   Grace to cover all my sin;
Let the healing streams abound,
   Make and keep me pure within:
Thou of life the fountain art;
   Freely let me take of thee;
Spring thou up within my heart,
   Rise to all eternity.

From John and Charles Wesley, *Hymns and Sacred Songs* (1740). Rev.
Henry Ward Beecher, brother of Harriet Beecher Stowe (q. v.) said 'I
would rather have written that hymn than to have all the fame of all
the kings that ever sat upon the earth.'

232

Christ, whose glory fills the skies,
   Christ, the true, the only light,
Sun of righteousness, arise,
   Triumph o'er the shades of night:
Dayspring from on high, be near;
Daystar, in my heart appear.

Dark and cheerless is the morn
   Unaccompanied by thee;
Joyless is the day's return,
   Till thy mercy's beams I see;
Till they inward light impart,
Glad my eyes, and warm my heart,

Visit then this soul of mine,
   Pierce the gloom of sin and grief:
Fill me, Radiancy divine,
   Scatter all my unbelief;
More and more thyself display,
Shining to the perfect day.

From John and Charles Wesley, *Hymns and Sacred Songs* (1740).
James Montgomery (q. v.) called this 'one of Charles Wesley's
loveliest progeny'.

233

Come, O thou Traveller unknown,
  Whom still I hold, but cannot see;
My company before is gone,
  And I am left alone with thee;
With thee all night I mean to stay,
And wrestle till the break of day.

I need not tell thee who I am,
  My misery or sin declare;
Thyself hast called me by my name;
  Look on thy hands, and read it there!
But who, I ask thee, who art thou?
Tell me thy name, and tell me now.

Yield to me now, for I am weak,
  But confident in self-despair;
Speak to my heart, in blessings speak,
  Be conquered by my instant prayer.
Speak, or thou never hence shalt move,
And tell me if thy name is Love.

'Tis Love! 'tis Love! Thou died'st for me!
  I hear thy whisper in my heart!
The morning breaks, the shadows flee;
  Pure universal love thou art;
To me, to all, thy mercies move;
Thy nature and thy name is Love.

'Wrestling Jacob' from *Hymns and Poems* (1742). Isaac Watts (q. v.)
thought this hymn 'worth all the verses I have written myself'.

234

Hark, how all the welkin rings!
'Glory to the King of Kings,
Peace on earth and mercy mild,
God and sinners reconciled.'

Joyful, all ye nations, rise,
Join the triumph of the skies;
Universal nature say
'Christ the Lord is born to-day.'

Christ by highest heaven adored,
Christ, the everlasting Lord,
Late in time behold him come
Offspring of the Virgin's womb.

Veiled in flesh, the Godhead see!
Hail the incarnate Deity!
Pleased as man with men to appear,
Jesus, our Emmanuel here!

Hail the heavenly Prince of Peace!
Hail the Sun of Righteousness!
Light and life to all he brings,
Risen with healing in his wings.

Mild he lays his glory by,
Born that man no more may die,
Born to raise the sons of earth,
Born to give them second birth!

Come, Desire of Nations, come,
Fix in us thy humble home;
Rise, the woman's conquering seed,
Bruise in us the serpent's head.

Now display thy saving power,
Ruined nature now restore,
Now in mystic union join
Thine to ours, and ours to thine.

One of the most popular hymns ever, this hymn was first published in
John and Charles Wesley's *Hymns and Sacred Songs* (1739). Originally
entitled 'Hymn for Christmas Day' it is better known with the altered
opening lines 'Hark the herald angels sing, /Glory to the new-born King'.

235

Love divine, all loves excelling,
   Joy of heav'n, to earth come down.
Fix in us thy humble dwelling,
   All thy faithful mercies crown.
Jesu, thou art all compassion,
   Pure unbounded love thou art;
Visit us with thy salvation,
   Enter every trembling heart.

Breathe, O breathe thy loving spirit
   Into every troubled breast!
Let us all in thee inherit,
   Let us find that second rest;
Take away our bent to sinning,
   Alpha and Omega be;
End of faith, as its beginning,
   Set our hearts at liberty.

Come, almighty to deliver,
   Let us all thy life receive,
Suddenly return, and never,
   Never more thy temples leave.
Thee we would be always blessing,
   Serve thee as thy hosts above,
Pray, and praise thee, without ceasing,
   Glory in thy perfect love.

Finish then thy new creation,
   Pure and sinless let us be;
Let us see thy great salvation,
   Perfectly restored in thee:
Changed from glory into glory,
   Till in heav'n we take our place,
Till we cast our crowns before thee,
   Lost in wonder, love, and praise!

From *Hymns for Those That Seek, and Those That Have Redemption* (1747)

236

And can it be, that I should gain
   An interest in the Saviour's blood?
Died He for me, who caused His pain –
   For me, who Him to death pursued?
Amazing love! How can it be
That Thou, my God, shouldst die for me?

'Tis mystery all! The Immortal dies:
   Who can explore His strange design?
In vain the first-born seraph tries
   To sound the depths of love divine.
'Tis mercy all! let earth adore,
Let angel minds inquire no more.

He left His Father's throne above, –
   So free, so infinite His grace, –
Emptied Himself of all but love,
   And bled for Adam's helpless race:
'Tis mercy all, immense and free;
For, O my God. it found out me!

Long my imprisoned spirit lay
   Fast bound in sin and nature's night;
Thine eye diffused a quickening ray, –
   I woke, the dungeon flamed with light;
My chains fell off, my heart was free;
I rose, went forth, and followed Thee.

Still the small inward voice I hear,
　That whispers all my sins forgiven;
Still the atoning Blood is near,
　That quenched the wrath of hostile heaven.
I feel the life His wounds impart;
I feel my Saviour in my heart.

No condemnation now I dread;
　Jesus, and all in Him, is mine!
Alive in Him, my living Head,
　And clothed in righteousness divine,
Bold I approach the eternal throne,
And claim the crown, through Christ my own.

First published in John Wesley's *Poems and Hymns* (1738)

JOHN WESLEY

(1703–91) English clergyman and poet

The son of the Rector of Epworth, Lincolnshire, and older
brother of Charles Wesley (q. v.), John Wesley founded the
Methodist movement and travelled thousands of miles each year
as an itinerant preacher. Best known as a translator of hymns, he
edited many collections including the *Methodist Hymn Book*.

237

Author of life divine,
　Who hast a table spread,
Furnished with mystic Wine
　And everlasting Bread,
Preserve the life thyself hast given,
And feed and train us up for heaven.

Our needy souls sustain
　　With fresh supplies of love,
Till all thy life we gain,
　　And all thy fulness prove,
And, strengthened by thy perfect grace,
Behold without a veil thy face.

From John and Charles Wesley's *Hymns on the Lord's Supper* (1745)

238

Verborgne Gottes Liebe du

Thou hidden Love of God, whose height,
　　Whose depth unfathomed, no man knows,
I see from far thy beauteous light,
　　Inly I sigh for thy repose;
My heart is pained, nor can it be
At rest till it finds rest in thee.

'Tis mercy all, that thou hast brought
　　My mind to seek her peace in thee;
Yet, while I seek but find thee not,
　　No peace my wandering soul shall see.
O when shall all my wanderings end,
And all my steps to thee-ward tend?

Thy secret voice invites me still
　　The sweetness of thy yoke to prove;
And fain I would; but, though my will
　　Seem fixed, yet wide my passions rove;
Yet hindrances strew all the way;
I aim at thee, yet from thee stray.

O Love! Thy sovereign aid impart
 To save me from low-thoughted care;
Chase this self-will through all my heart,
 Through all its latent mazes there;
Make me thy duteous child, that I
Ceaseless may 'Abba, Father' cry.

Translated from the German of Gerhard Tersteegen in John Wesley's
first hymnbook, *The Charles-town Collection* (1737). Oliver Wendell
Holmes (q. v.) and Emerson (q. v.) both thought this the greatest hymn
in the English language.

WALT WHITMAN

(1819–92) American poet and journalist

Born in Long Island, Whitman worked successively as a school-teacher, journalist and novelist. During the American Civil War he was a clerk in Washington and a volunteer nurse. An admirer of Emerson (q. v.) he is best known for his book of poems, *Leaves of Grass.*

239

All the past we leave behind:
We take up the task eternal, and the burden, and the lesson,
Conquering, holding, daring, venturing, so we go the unknown ways,
 Pioneers! O pioneers!

Not for delectations sweet,
Not the riches safe and palling, not for us the tame enjoyment;
Never must you be divided, in our ranks you move united,
 Pioneers! O pioneers!

All the pulses of the world,
All the joyous, all the sorrowing, these are of us, they are with us;
We to-day's procession heading, we the route for travel clearing,
 Pioneers! O pioneers!

On and on the compact ranks,
With accessions ever waiting, we must never yield or falter,
Through the battle, through defeat, moving yet and never stopping,
    Pioneers! O pioneers!

From 'Pioneers, O Pioneers' in Leaves of Grass (1865)

JOHN GREENLEAF WHITTIER

(1807–92) American poet and journalist

Born in Massachusetts, Whittier was a Quaker and an ardent
anti-slavery campaigner. He was editor of *New England Review*
and *Pennsylvania Freeman*.

240

Dear Lord and Father of mankind,
    Forgive our foolish ways!
Re-clothe us in our rightful mind,
In purer lives thy service find,
    In deeper reverence praise.

In simple trust like theirs who heard,
    Beside the Syrian sea,
The gracious calling of the Lord,
Let us, like them, without a word
    Rise up and follow thee.

O Sabbath rest by Galilee!
    O calm of hills above,
Where Jesus knelt to share with thee
The silence of eternity,
    Interpreted by love!

With that deep hush subduing all
    Our words and works that drown
The tender whisper of thy call,
As noiseless let thy blessing fall
    As fell thy manna down.

Drop thy still dews of quietness,
  Till all our strivings cease;
Take from our souls the strain and stress,
And let our ordered lives confess
  The beauty of thy peace.

Breathe through the heats of our desire
  Thy coolness and thy balm;
Let sense be dumb, let flesh retire;
Speak through the earthquake, wind, and fire,
  O still small voice of calm!

From 'The Brewing of Soma' in *Complete Poetical Works* (1876)

241

All as God wills, who wisely heeds
  To give or to withhold,
And knoweth more of all my needs
  Than all my prayers have told!

Enough that blessings undeserved
  Have marked my erring track;
That wheresoe'er my feet have swerved
  His chastening turned me back;

That more and more a providence
  Of love is understood,
Making the springs of time and sense
  Sweet with eternal good;

That death seems but a covered way
  Which opens into light,
Wherein no blinded child can stray
  Beyond the Father's sight;

That care and trial seem at last,
  Through memory's sunset air,
Like mountain ranges overpast,
  In purple distance fair;

That all the jarring notes of life
   Seem blending in a psalm,
And all the angles of its strife
   Slow rounding into calm.

And so the shadows fall apart,
   And so the west winds play;
And all the windows of my heart
   I open to the day.

From 'My Psalm' in *The Panorama* (1856)

242

Immortal love, for ever full,
   For ever flowing free,
For ever shared, for ever whole,
   A never-ebbing sea.

Our outward lips confess the name
   All other names above;
Love only knoweth whence it came,
   And comprehendeth love.

We may not climb the heavenly steeps,
   To bring the Lord Christ down;
In vain we search the lowest deeps,
   For him no depths can drown.

But warm, sweet, tender, even yet
   A present help is he;
And faith hath still its Olivet,
   And love its Galilee.

The healing of his seamless dress
   Is by our beds of pain;
We touch him in life's throng and press,
   And we are whole again.

Through him the first fond prayers are said
   Our lips of childhood frame;
The last low whispers of our dead
   Are burdened with his name.

O Lord and Master of us all,
   Whate'er our name or sign,
We own thy sway, we hear thy call,
   We test our lives by thine.

From *Hymnal Companion* (1890)

243

O brother man, fold to thy heart thy brother!
   Where pity dwells, the peace of God is there;
To worship rightly is to love each other,
   Each smile a hymn, each kindly deed a prayer.

For he whom Jesus loved hath truly spoken:
   The holier worship which he deigns to bless
Restores the lost, and binds the spirit broken,
   And feeds the widow and the fatherless.

Follow with reverent steps the great example
   Of him whose holy work was doing good;
So shall the wide earth seem our Father's temple,
   Each loving life a psalm of gratitude.

Then shall all shackles fall; the stormy clangour
   Of wild war-music o'er the earth shall cease;
Love shall tread out the baleful fire of anger,
   And in its ashes plant the tree of peace.

Based on James 1:27

GEORGE WITHER

(1588–1667) English poet and pamphleteer

Imprisoned by James I for writing a political pamphlet, Wither
served as a Captain of Horse under Charles II against the
Covenanters, was a Major-General under Cromwell and was
later imprisoned in both Newgate and the Tower of London
for his writings.

244

Behold the sun, that seemed but now
  Enthronèd overhead,
Beginning to decline below
  This globe whereon we tread;
And he, whom yet we look upon
  With comfort and delight,
Will quite depart from hence anon,
  And leave us to the night.

Thus time, unheeded, steals away
  The life which nature gave;
Thus are our bodies every day
  Declining to the grave;
Thus from us all those pleasures fly
  Whereon we set our heart;
And when the night of death draws nigh,
  Thus will they all depart.

Lord! though the sun forsake our sight,
  And mortal hopes are vain,
Let still thine everlasting light
  Within our souls remain;
And in the nights of our distress
  Vouchsafe those rays divine,
Which from the Sun of Righteousness
  For ever brightly shine!

From *Hallelujah* (1641)

245

The Lord of heaven confess;
　On high his glory raise:
Him let all angels bless,
　Him all his armies praise.
　　Him glorify
　　　Sun, moon, and stars;
　　　Ye higher spheres,
　　And cloudy sky.

Praise God from earth below,
　Ye dragons, and ye deeps:
Fire, hail, clouds, wind, and snow,
　Whom in command he keeps.
　　Praise ye his name,
　　　Hills great and small,
　　　Trees low and tall,
　　Beasts wild and tame.

O let God's name be praised
　Above both earth and sky;
For he his saints hath raised,
　And set their horn on high;
　　Yea, they that are
　　　Of Israel's race;
　　　Are in his grace,
　And ever, dear.

Based on Psalm 148, from *The Psalms of David* (1632)

246

To God, with heart and cheerful voice,
　A triumph song we sing;
And with true thankful hearts rejoice
　In our almighty King;
Yea, to his glory we record,
　Who were but dust and clay,
What honour he did us afford
　On his ascending day.

Each door and everlasting gate
　To him hath lifted been;
And in a glorious wise thereat
　Our King is entered in;
Whom if to follow we regard,
　With ease we safely may,
For he hath all the means prepared,
　And made an open way.

Then follow, follow on apace,
    And let us not forgo
Our Captain, till we win the place
    That he hath scaled unto:
And for his honour, let our voice
    A shout so hearty make,
The heavens may at our mirth rejoice,
    And earth and hell may shake.

247

Come, O come in pious lays
Sound we God-Almighty's praise.
Hither bring, in one consent,
Heart and voice and instrument.
Strike the viol, touch the lute
Let not tongue nor string be mute:
    Nor a creature dumb be found
    That hath either voice or sound.

Lowly pipe, ye worms that creep
On the earth, or in the deep;
Loud-aloft your voices strain,
Beasts, and monsters of the main;
Birds, your warbling treble sing,
Clouds, your peals of thunder ring.
    Sun and moon, exalted higher
    And bright stars, augment this choir.

Come, ye sons of human race,
In this chorus take a place;
And, amid the mortal-throng
Be you masters of the song.
Let in praise of God the sound
Run a never-ending round,
    That our song of praise may be
    Everlasting, as is He.

From earth's vast and hollow womb
Music's deepest bass may come;
To this consort, when we sing,
Whistling winds, your descants bring.
That our song may overclimb
All the bounds of space and time.
    And ascend from sphere to sphere
    To the great Almighty's ear.

So, from heaven, on earth, he shall
Let his gracious blessings fall,
And this huge wide orb, we see,
Shall one choir, one temple be,
Where, in such a praise-full tone,
We will sing what he hath done.
    Then, O come, in pious lays
    Sound we God-Almighty's praise.

✥ ✥ ✥

CHRISTOPHER WORDSWORTH

(1807–85) English clergyman and religious writer

Nephew of the poet William Wordsworth (q. v.) and son of the
Rector of Lambeth, Christopher Wordsworth became a Fellow
of Trinity College, Cambridge, Headmaster of Harrow School,
a Canon of Westminster Cathedral and later Bishop of Lincoln.

248

See the Conqueror mounts in triumph,
    See the King in royal state
Riding on the clouds his chariot
    To his heavenly palace gate;
Hark! the choirs of angel voices
    Joyful Alleluias sing,
And the portals high are lifted
    To receive their heavenly King.

Who is this that comes in glory,
    With the trump of jubilee?
Lord of battles, God of armies,
    He has gained the victory;
He who on the Cross did suffer,
    He who from the grave arose,
He has vanquished sin and Satan,
    He by death has spoiled his foes.

He has raised our human nature
    On the clouds to God's right hand;
There we sit in heavenly places,
    There with him in glory stand.
Jesus reigns, adored by angels;
    Man with God is on the throne;
Mighty Lord, in thine Ascension
    We by faith behold our own.

See him who is gone before us
    Heavenly mansions to prepare,
See him who is ever pleading
    For us with prevailing prayer,
See him who with sound of trumpet
    And with his angelic train,
Summoning the world to judgement,
    On the clouds will come again.

Glory be to God the Father;
    Glory be to God the Son,
Dying, risen, ascending for us,
    Who the heavenly realm has won;
Glory to the Holy Spirit:
    To One God in Persons Three
Glory both in earth and heaven,
    Glory, endless glory be.

        From *The Holy Year* (1862)

249

Hark! the sound of holy voices,
    Chanting at the crystal sea
Alleluia, Alleluia,
    Alleluia, Lord, to thee:
Multitude, which none can number,
    Like the stars in glory stands,
Clothed in white apparel, holding
    Palms of victory in their hands.

Patriarch, and holy prophet,
    Who prepared the way of Christ,
King, apostle, saint, confessor,
    Martyr, and evangelist,
Saintly maiden, godly matron,
    Widows who have watched to prayer,
Joined in holy concert, singing
    To the Lord of all, are there.

They have come from tribulation,
    And have washed their robes in Blood,
Washed them in the Blood of Jesus;
    Tried they were, and firm they stood:
Mocked, imprisoned, stoned, tormented,
    Sawn asunder, slain with sword,
They have conquered death and Satan
    By the might of Christ the Lord.

Marching with thy Cross their banner,
    They have triumphed following
Thee, the Captain of Salvation,
    Thee their Saviour and their King:
Gladly, Lord, with thee they suffered;
    Gladly, Lord, with thee they died,
And by death to life immortal
    They were born, and glorified.

Now they reign in heavenly glory,
 Now they walk in golden light,
Now they drink, as from a river,
 Holy bliss and infinite;
Love and peace they taste for ever
 And all truth and knowledge see
In the beatific vision
 Of the blessèd Trinity.

God of God, the One-begotten,
 Light of Light, Emmanuel,
In whose Body joined together
 All the saints for ever dwell;
Pour upon us of thy fulness,
 That we may for evermore
God the Father, God the Son, and
 God the Holy Ghost adore.

WILLIAM WORDSWORTH

(1770–1850) English poet

Born in Cumbria, Wordsworth's first important collection of poems, *Lyrical Ballads*, written jointly with Coleridge (q. v.), was published in 1799. For many years Stamp Distributor for Westmorland (1813–42), he succeeded Southey as Poet Laureate in 1843.

250

Stern daughter of the Voice of God!
 O Duty! if that name thou love,
Who art a light to guide, a rod
 To check the erring, and reprove;
Thou, who art victory and law
When empty terrors overawe,
From empty temptations dost set free,
And calm'st the weary strife of frail humanity.

Serene will be our days and bright,
   And happy will our nature be,
When love is an unerring light,
   And joy its own security;
And they a blissful course may hold
Even now, who, not unwisely bold,
Live in the spirit of this creed,
Yet seek thy firm support, according to their need.

Stern lawgiver! yet thou dost wear
   The Godhead's most benignant grace;
Nor know we anything so fair
   As is the smile upon thy face:
Flowers laugh before thee on their beds
And fragrance in thy footing treads;
Thou dost preserve the stars from wrong:
And the most ancient heavens, through thee, are fresh and strong.

To humbler functions, aweful power,
   I call thee! I myself commend
Unto thy guidance from this hour;
   O let my weakness have an end!
Give unto me, made lowly wise,
The spirit of self-sacrifice;
The confidence of reason give,
And in the light of truth thy bondman let me live!

From 'Ode to Duty'

251

Not seldom, clad in radiant vest,
Deceitfully goes forth the Morn;
Not seldom Evening in the west
Sinks smilingly forsworn.

The smoothest seas will sometimes prove,
To the confiding Bark, untrue;
And, if she trust the stars above
They can be treacherous too.

The umbrageous Oak, in pomp outspread,
Full oft, when storms the welkin rend,
Draws lightning down upon the head
It promised to defend.

But Thou art true, incarnate Lord,
Who didst vouchsafe for man to die;
Thy smile is sure, Thy plighted word
No change can falsify!

I bent before Thy gracious throne,
And asked for peace on suppliant knee;
And peace was given, – nor peace alone,
But faith sublimed to ecstasy!

No. 5 of 'Inscriptions Supposed to be Found In and Near a Hermit's
Cell, 1818' in *Poetical Works* (1837)

252

Blest are the moments, doubly blest,
That, drawn from this one hour of rest,
Are with a ready heart bestowed
Upon the service of our God!

Each field is then a hallowed spot,
An altar is in each man's cot,
A church in every grove that spreads
Its living roof above our heads.

Look up to heaven! the industrious sun
Already half his race hath run;
He cannot halt or go astray,
But our immortal spirits may.

Lord, since his rising in the east,
If we have faltered or transgressed,
Guide, from thy love's abundant source,
What yet remains of this day's course;

Help with thy grace, through life's short day,
Our upward and our downward way;
And glorify for us the west,
When we shall sink to final rest.

From 'The Labourer's Noon-day Hymn' (1834)

SIR HENRY WOTTON

(1568–1639) English diplomat, writer and poet

A close friend of Donne (q. v.), Sir Henry Wotton was successively Agent and Secretary to the Earl of Essex, James I's Ambassador to Venice and Provost of Eton. He is famously quoted as saying 'An ambassador is an honest man, sent to lie abroad for the good of his country.'

253

How happy is he born and taught,
   That serveth not another's will;
Whose armour is his honest thought,
   And simple truth his utmost skill.

Whose passions not his masters are;
   Whose soul is still, prepared for death,
Untied unto the world by care
   Of public fame or private breath;

Who God doth late and early pray
   More of his grace than goods to lend;
And walks with man from day to day
   As with a brother and a friend.

This man is freed from servile bands
Of hope to rise, or fear to fall;
Lord of himself, though not of lands.
And, having nothing, yet hath all.

From *Reliquiae Wottonianae* (1651)

INDEX OF FIRST LINES